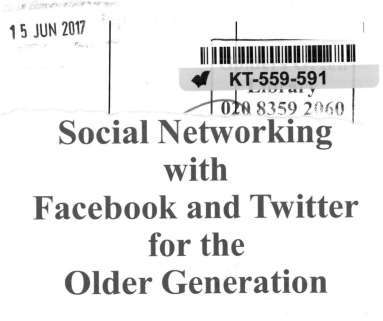

Social Networking with Facebook and Twitter for the Older Generation

Jim Gatenby

BERNARD BABANI (publishing) LTD
The Grampians
Shepherds Bush Road
London W6 7NF
England

www.babanibooks.com

Please Note

Although every care has been taken with the production of this book to ensure that all information is correct at the time of writing and that any projects, designs, modifications and/ or programs, etc., contained herewith, operate in a correct and safe manner and also that any components specified are normally available in Great Britain, the Publishers and Author do not accept responsibility in any way for the failure (including fault in design) of any project, design, modification or program to work correctly or to cause damage to any equipment that it may be connected to or used in conjunction with, or in respect of any other damage or injury that may be so caused, nor do the Publishers accept responsibility in any way for the failure to obtain specified components.

Notice is also given that if equipment that is still under warranty is modified in any way or used or connected with home-built equipment then that warranty may be void.

First Published – March 2017

British Library Cataloguing in Publication Data:

A catalogue record for this book is available from the British Library

ISBN 978-0-85934-764-8

Cover Design by Gregor Arthur

Printed and bound in Great Britain for Bernard Babani (publishing) Ltd

About this Book

Social networking Websites like Facebook and Twitter allow people to share news, photos and live video calls with friends and family all over the world. Research has shown that this can be very beneficial as well as enjoyable.

The latest small, portable, smartphones, tablets and laptop computers mean that you can keep in touch with your contacts wherever you are. The material in this book applies to the hugely successful iPhone and iPad and the top selling Android range. The material is also intended for users of the Microsoft Windows operating system on smartphones, tablets, laptops and desktop computers.

The book describes downloading and installing *app*s, i.e. applications or software, for Facebook and Twitter. Signing up and entering your personal details is also covered, enabling you to communicate with like-minded people to share news, photos and live video calls, etc. Facebook and Twitter now allow messages to include ready-made, amusing images (known as *emojis*) and video clips selected free from online libraries, as well as *broadcasting* live video.

Also covered are the built-in *privacy settings* to control who can see the information you post on Facebook and Twitter.

Twitter is the second most popular social network, allowing short messages or *Tweets* of up to 140 characters, to be posted on the Internet. As described in detail, you can *follow* the Tweets of celebrities, etc., post your own Tweets, join an online debate or promote a business, or campaign, etc. You can also use Twitter to exchange private *Direct Messages* with selected people or groups.

This book is written in simple language and avoiding jargon to help the new user to get started with Facebook and Twitter with confidence and security.

About the Author

Jim Gatenby trained as a Chartered Mechanical Engineer and initially worked at Rolls-Royce Ltd using computers in the analysis of jet engine performance. He obtained a Master of Philosophy degree in Mathematical Education by research at Loughborough University of Technology and taught mathematics and computing in school for many years before becoming a full-time author. His most recent teaching posts included Head of Computer Studies and Information Technology Co-ordinator. The author has written over forty books, including many of the titles in the highly successful 'Older Generation' series from Bernard Babani (publishing) Ltd.

Trademarks

Android is a trademark or registered trademark of Google Inc. iOS, iPhone and iPad are trademarks or registered trademarks of Apple Inc. Microsoft Windows is a trademark or registered trademark of Microsoft Corporation. Facebook and Facebook Messenger are registered trademarks of Facebook, Inc. Twitter is a registered trademark of Twitter, Inc.

All other brand and product names used in this book are recognized as trademarks or registered trademarks of their respective companies.

Acknowledgements

As usual I would like to thank my wife Jill for her continued support during the preparation of this book and our sons David and Richard for providing many of the photos. Also The Basement Thai Restaurant, Ashbourne for the use of their Facebook page and Michael Babani for making this project possible.

Contents

5

6

Facebook: An Overview

What is Facebook?

Facebook is the world's most popular *social networking* Web site with over a billion users. Like Twitter discussed later in this book, Facebook allows people to communicate with friends and family anywhere in the world. You can exchange latest news and information, photos and videos and keep in touch quickly and easily. Networks like Facebook and Twitter can also be used to promote a business or gather support for a cause which matters to you.

Privacy and Security are Easily Protected

Facebook allows you to enter *personal data*, so you can make contact and, if you choose to, make *friends* with like-minded people. Care is needed when *posting* i.e. uploading and displaying personal information on Facebook, which is effectively a world-wide noticeboard. Fortunately you can control who sees your data using privacy settings known as *audience selectors*. These pop up on menus, as shown below, launched from icons at the side of pieces of data.

Who should see this?	
🌐 Public	
👥 Friends	✓
🔒 Only Me	

Age is No Barrier

Although it's sometimes said that social networks are the exclusive preserve of the young, in reality they are used by people of all ages. In fact, official statistics show that more than half the users of social networks are aged over 35. Perhaps surprisingly, Facebook has even had some users well past their hundredth birthday!

Facebook Is Easy to Use

You don't need to be a "geek" or a computer wizard to use Facebook. As described in this book, all of the tasks are performed using simple menus and icons. Using Facebook is very similar on all types of computer, phones and tablets.

Facebook is Free

You don't have to pay to use Facebook – the company derives its income from advertising. You just need to be at least 13 years of age and have a computer, tablet or smartphone connected to the Internet, together with a valid e-mail account.

Always Up to date

Some people use Facebook at home or at work on a desktop or laptop computer. Then when they're travelling they use a smartphone or tablet. Since Facebook is a Web site, any new posts of messages, photos, etc., are always available on all of your devices.

As shown on the next page, Facebook can be used on all of the different types of computer.

iPad Tablet   **Android Smartphone**

Windows Desktop PC

Facebook is used in a similar way on all of the various
types of computer shown above, although there are some
differences in the screen layouts and the positions of some
of the icons, as shown on pages 8, 9 and 10.

Use Facebook Anywhere

Facebook is widely used on mobile devices as shown below on an Android smartphone. So you can use Facebook anywhere — when you're out and about or at home perhaps on a desktop or laptop machine. If you see something interesting on your travels you could take a photo or video with your phone and post it as a *status update* with a message. The update will then be available to your friends, depending on your *privacy settings*. These are the *audience selectors*, discussed later, used to determine who sees what.

Why Should Older People Use Facebook?

Facebook was founded in 2004 by students at Harvard University. It was intended to help new students to get to know each other. So how can Facebook be relevant to older people, for whom this book is intended?

Facebook can be particularly helpful to older people for the following reasons:

- Many older people live alone and may be separated from children and grandchildren who may live a long way from their roots — overseas perhaps. Facebook can keep families in touch.

- Some older people are prevented by mobility problems from travelling to see friends and family. Facebook can provide face-to-face conversations without leaving home, with just a tap or a click — without the need to travel.

- Facebook searches for people who may share your background such as school or work, etc., so it can help to renew long-lost friendships.

- Older people usually have more time to learn new skills and become highly competent with activities such as Facebook.

- Older people, especially if retired and less active, can benefit from stimulating mental activities like computing in general and Facebook in particular.

Features of Facebook

This section lists the functions of some of the main Facebook features. Detailed step-by-step examples of their use are given in later chapters.

Timeline

A listing of events in your life in chronological order, including photos, updates and posts from friends.

Profile

Includes a photo to identify you and a description of your interests, hobbies, schools, employment, etc. Facebook uses this information to suggest people with similar backgrounds to you to invite to be your Facebook *friends*.

Friend

A person you've agreed to share news and information with on Facebook. Friends can be placed in categories and these categories used to control who sees your information.

✿ Close Friends	
✿ London Area	
✿ Family	✓
♟ Relations	

You can send and receive *Friend requests* and these may be accepted, declined or ignored.

News Feed

Also known as your Home Page, where the latest news, messages, photos and videos from your friends appear.

Update or Status Update

A post or message to friends saying what you're doing, etc. A photo, video or Web link can be included. Friends can reply by tapping or clicking **Like**, writing a **Comment** or **Sharing** with their own friends.

Your status update appears on your friends' News Feeds and also on your own News Feed and Timeline. Although often very brief, the text of an update can actually be up to a mammoth 63,206 characters long, unlike Twitter, with its 140 character limit.

Events

This feature allows you to inform friends of future events and social occasions, with details such as the time and location of the event.

Groups

This is a collection of Facebook users with a common interest, to share information and join in discussions. Groups may be set up by individuals, clubs, companies and other organisations.

Photos

This feature allows you to build up albums of photos. People in photos can be *tagged*, so that others can see who is in the photo. The people who are tagged are notified of the tag and a copy of the photo sent to their Facebook page.

Facebook on Different Platforms

Desktops and Laptops

Facebook is a Web site and so can be accessed by typing its address, **facebook.com**, into a *Web browser*. Popular browsers are Internet Explorer, Microsoft Edge, Safari, Google Chrome and Firefox.

Shown below is a screenshot from the Facebook Web site running on a Windows 10 Desktop PC.

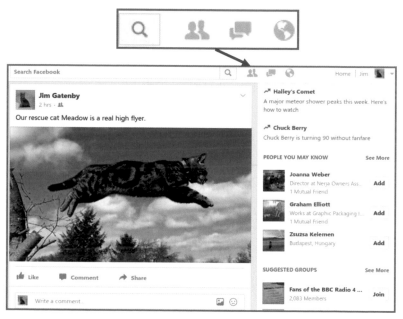

The Facebook Web Site on a Desktop PC

The icons in the top screenshot above control some of the main features of Facebook and are described shortly. Smartphones and tablets can also access the Facebook Web site using a browser such as Google Chrome or Safari.

Smartphones and Tablets

Special Facebook *apps* have been developed for smartphones and tablets, taking account of the smaller screen sizes of mobile devices. Apps are computer programs, i.e. software available in the app stores such as the Google Play Store for Android devices and the App Store for iPhones and iPads. Downloading the Facebook apps is discussed in the next chapter.

iPhone and iPad

Shown below is a status update posted on the News Feed of an iPad. The iPhone version is the same only smaller.

The Facebook App on an iPad

Android Smartphones and Tablets

Shown below is a status update posted on the News Feed of Android smartphone.

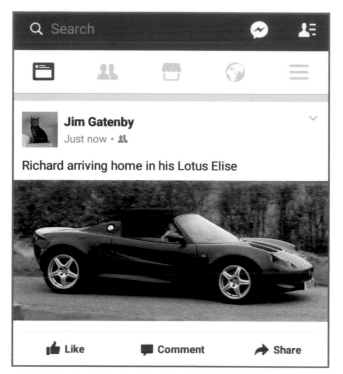

The Facebook App on an Android Smartphone

Facebook on an Android tablet is very similar to the smartphone version shown above apart from a slight difference in the layout of the icons at the top of the screen, as shown below.

The Layout of Facebook Icons on an Android Tablet

Using Facebook

Facebook is designed to be used in basically the same way on all platforms — smartphone, tablet, laptop or desktop. This similarity also applies to all the common operating systems — Android, iOS (iPad and iPhone) and Windows. The same icons are used, as shown below, although there are differences in colour and the layout on the screen.

The icons shown below launch some of the main Facebook features and were captured from an Android tablet. The icons are "greyed out" or faint when not selected.

The fact that Facebook is used in a similar way on all platforms makes it easy to switch seamlessly between the different types of computer — smartphone, desktop, etc.

Display your News Feed

View Friend Requests

Display Notifications of updates and activity by friends on your Facebook page

Open a menu to display the main Facebook features — Timeline, Groups, Events, etc.

Search for people, friends, events

Switch to the Timeline and User Profile

Launch the Facebook Messenger App

Promoting a Business

Setting up your own Facebook *Page* to promote a business or charitable cause amongst your Facebook friends and contacts is free. Large companies pay for separate advertisements on Facebook targeted at particular audiences. Shown below is a Facebook Page for a local restaurant. This includes a map showing the restaurant's location, contact details, opening times, photos, live videos of special evenings and customer reviews.

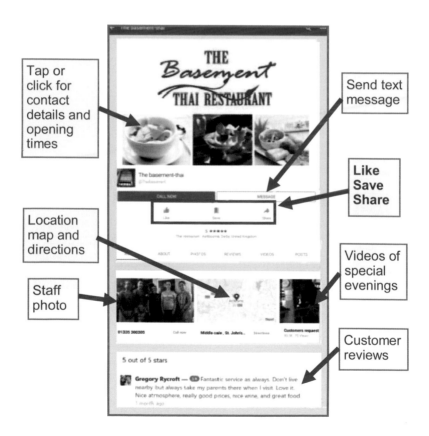

Tap or click for contact details and opening times

Send text message

Like Save Share

Location map and directions

Staff photo

Videos of special evenings

Customer reviews

Facebook Messenger

This is a free additional Facebook app, often referred to as simply Messenger. It provides all of the messaging facilities previously built into the main Facebook app. Unlike the *status updates* discussed earlier, a message is sent between specific Facebook users, rather than posted to all friends, etc., depending on the privacy settings.

Some of the main features of Facebook Messenger are:

- *Chatting* to individuals or groups by sending and receiving *instant text messages*.
- Live voice conversations, including face-to-face *video* on devices with suitable Web cam facilities.
- Messenger calls are free when using a Wi-Fi network such as a home router. A 3G or 4G phone service may make a charge on your data plan.

So, for example, anyone in England with grandchildren in, say, Australia or Hong Kong can see and talk to them in real time without charge, when using a Wi-Fi Internet connection.

Key Points: Facebook: An Overview

- Facebook keeps people in touch with friends and family <u>anywhere in the world</u>, by posting text, photos, voice and video messages on each other's Facebook News Feeds.

- Facebook can be used to promote a business, etc.

- Facebook is free and can be accessed directly from the **facebook.com** Web site or using *apps* designed specially for tablets and smartphones.

- Facebook can be used by <u>people of all ages </u>to make *friends* and communicate with people posting similar backgrounds or interests on their *Profile*.

- Facebook is *easy to use* and works in a similar way <u>on all types of computer </u>— on the move or in the home or office.

- Facebook is a Web site, so the data is always up-to-date on all the machines you use.

- *Audience selectors* are privacy settings which should be used to control <u>who sees what data</u>.

- Facebook Messenger is a separate app providing instant text, voice and video messaging which is free when using Wi-Fi or may incur a charge over a 3G/4G mobile phone service.

2

Getting Set Up

Introduction

Facebook is a Web site, a collection of pages of information stored on a computer on the Internet. Therefore to access Facebook you need a smartphone, tablet, laptop or desktop computer connected to the Internet.

In the home, office or college the Internet connection is made via a *local network* based on a *Wi-Fi wireless router*. To access Facebook on the move, where there is no Wi-Fi, you need a smartphone or tablet which connects to the Internet through a *3G* or *4G cell phone network*, such as EE, Three, O2 and Vodafone. While smartphones have 3G or 4G connectivity built-in as standard, tablets with this facility are available but more expensive than *Wi-Fi-only* tablets.

The Facebook App vs the Facebook Web Site

The Facebook *app* (application) can be freely downloaded from your app store and saved on your computer. This chapter shows you how you can set up the app to get you started using Facebook quickly and easily.

Facebook can also be run in a *Web browser* and this approach is also discussed in this chapter. The features and methods of operating Facebook are basically the same whether the app or a Web browser is used.

Using the Facebook App

Android and iOS

This section applies to Android tablets and smartphones and iOS (iPhone and iPad) devices.

Special Facebook apps have been designed to work with Android and iOS smartphones and tablets with their smaller screens compared with desktops and laptops.

If the Facebook app is already installed on your device, its icon will appear on your Home screen, as shown on the right.

Facebook

If your smartphone or tablet does not already have the Facebook app installed, it's available free from your app store, as discussed on the next few pages.

Installing the App: Android Smartphones and Tablets

The Facebook app is installed from the **Google Play Store** after tapping the icon shown on the right and entering **Facebook** in the **Play Store** search bar. Tap the Facebook icon shown on the left below, then tap **INSTALL** to download and save the app on your device.

Installing the App: iPhones and iPads

Tap the **App Store** icon shown on the right and then enter Facebook in the **App Store** search bar.

Then tap **GET** shown below to install Facebook on your iPhone or iPad. (If Facebook is already installed on a device, an **OPEN** button appears instead of **GET** shown below).

The Facebook Messenger app, shown on the right above and at the bottom of page 16, is discussed in Chapter 7.

Launching Facebook from the App

Installing the Faccbook app places an icon on the Home screen as shown in the extracts below. Tap the icon to launch the Facebook app.

Android

iOS (iPhone and iPad)

The Facebook App: Windows 10

A free Facebook app is available in the **Store** in Windows 10, for smartphones and tablets, as well as desktop and laptop computers. Users of laptop and desktop computers may prefer the more traditional Web browser approach to using Facebook, rather than the app, and this is discussed shortly.

Installing the App: Windows 10

Tap or click the **Store** tile, shown on the right, on the Start Menu. Then enter **Facebook** in the **Store** search bar. Icons for various Facebook-related apps are displayed, including the main Facebook app shown on the left below.

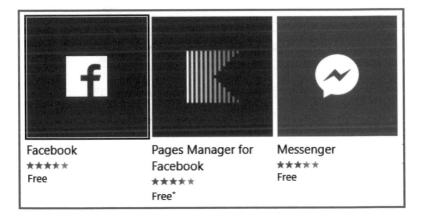

Facebook
★★★★★
Free

Pages Manager for Facebook
★★★★★
Free*

Messenger
★★★★★
Free

Tap or click the Facebook icon shown above on the left, then tap or click **Get** to install the Facebook app on your device.

This Facebook app can also be used on Windows 8.1.

The Facebook icon appears as shown below in the All Apps list on the Start Menu. Tap the icon to launch Facebook.

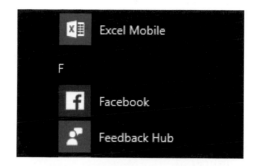

Alternatively touch and and hold or right-click the Facebook icon shown above then select **Pin to Start** shown below.

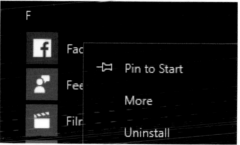

This places a *tile* for Facebook on the Windows 10 Start Menu as shown below on the right. The tile can then be used to launch Facebook.

Where to now?

To learn how to launch Facebook in a *Web browser*, instead of the app, carry on reading this chapter, which does get a little more complicated.

To get started straightaway using Facebook via the app, as discussed on the last few pages, jump ahead now to Chapter 3 and start building your Profile. Later, when you're more familiar with Facebook, you may wish to return to page 21 and check out the Web browser approach.

The Web Browser

www.facebook.com

This is the full version of the Facebook Web site traditionally used on laptop and desktop computers, before the proliferation of smartphones and tablets in recent years.

The full Web site can also be used on some tablet computers with large screens. Facebook is launched by typing its *Web address*, **www.facebook.com**, into a Web browser as shown below.

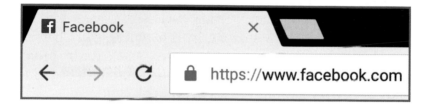

Popular Web browsers include Google Chrome and Apple Safari as shown below. These are installed by default on new smartphones or tablets or as free downloads from the Internet for laptops and desktops. Windows 10 users get the Microsoft Edge browser pre-installed on their device.

After entering the Web address **www.facebook.com** into the browser and tapping or clicking **Enter**, **Go**, etc., this opens the full Facebook Web site as shown in the example below.

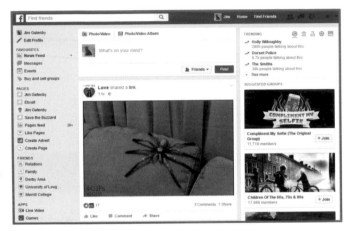

The full Web site www.facebook.com

The full Web site **www.facebook.com** is still an excellent way to run Facebook on desktops, laptops and some tablets.

As shown above, there is a great deal of data and images on the Web page at **www.facebook.com** — too much to be displayed on the small screen of a smartphone and some tablets.

I have also used the full Web site **www.facebook.com** on my iPad and on several Android tablets. These include the Nexus 7, Nexus 9 and the Hudl2. However, when I entered **www.facebook.com** into the Web browser on the Kindle Fire tablet, the Web site **m.facebook.com** opened by default. This is the *Facebook Mobile Web site* intended for smartphones and tablets, discussed on pages 23 onwards.

The Facebook Mobile Web Site

When you type **www.facebook.com** into Google Chrome on an Android smartphone and into Safari on an iPhone, like the Kindle Fire tablet described at the bottom of the previous page, it opens **m.facebook.com**, the Facebook Mobile Web site.

Many people are no doubt happy running Facebook from the free app installed from their app store. However, it has been claimed that the Facebook app runs slowly. Also that the app can drain the battery quickly.

So the Facebook Mobile Web site may be a better option than the Facebook app on smartphones and tablets. However, not all implementations of the Android operating system are the same on all Android devices from different manufacturers. You might wish to experiment to find the best way to run Facebook on your particular smartphone (or tablet).

Setting Up Facebook Mobile

So you could try setting up Facebook Mobile as discussed below and on the next few pages. The main steps are:

- Delete the original Facebook app
- Open the Facebook Mobile Web site:
  http://m.facebook.com
- Place a new Facebook icon on the screen

Deleting the original app is not essential but may avoid confusion and create a less-cluttered Home screen.

Deleting the Original Facebook App

If the Facebook app is pre-installed on your device, its icon or tile will be present on the Home screen as shown below.

Facebook

Facebook

Facebook

Android Devices

Touch and hold the Facebook icon then drag and drop the icon over **Uninstall**.

iOS (iPhone and iPad)

Tap and hold the Facebook icon, then tap the cross which appears at the top left of the icon as shown on the right. Then tap **Delete** from the pop-up menu. Finally tap the Home button to stop all the icons "jiggling" .

Facebook

Windows 10

Touch and hold or right-click the tile on Start or the icon in the All Apps list. Then select **Uninstall** from the menu which pops up, as shown below.

Opening the Mobile Web Site

Open your Web browser such as Google Chrome, Apple Safari or Microsoft Edge by tapping or clicking one of the icons shown on page 21. Then enter **m.facebook.com** into the search bar of the browser. (**https://** shown below is added automatically). Finally tap or click **Enter** or **Go** or the arrow key shown on the right, on the on-screen keyboard on an Android tablet.

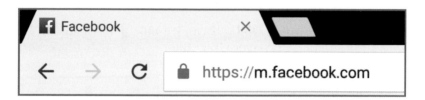

The Facebook Mobile screen opens, as shown below on an Android tablet. Obviously this is much more compact than the full Facebook Web site shown on page 22.

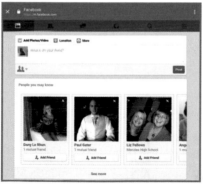

Mobile Web site m.facebook.com

Although primarily designed for smartphones and tablets, the mobile Web site can also be run in a Web browser on desktop and laptop computers.

Adding a Facebook Icon for a Web Site

(This section applies to both the full Web site **www.facebook.com** and the mobile site **m.facebook.com**)

Typing **www.facebook.com** or **m.facebook.com** into a Web browser is one way to launch Facebook. However, it's quicker and easier to tap or click an icon or tile on the screen. Adding a Facebook icon is discussed below.

Android Devices

Open either the full or the mobile Facebook Web site in a Web browser such as Google Chrome, as just discussed.

Tap the 3-dot menu button at the top right of the Facebook screen, as shown on the right. Then select **Add to Home screen** shown below on the left.

Find in page

Add to Home screen

Request desktop site

Add to Home screen

Facebook

CANCEL   ADD

Finally select **ADD** shown above on the right to place an icon for Facebook on the Home screen, as shown below.

Facebook   Excel   OneDrive

iOS (iPhone and iPad)

Open either the full or the mobile Web site in a Web browser such as Safari as shown below. Then tap the **Share** icon shown on the right and below.

Next select **Add to Home Screen** as shown on the right, from the **Share** panel which opens, as shown in the extract below.

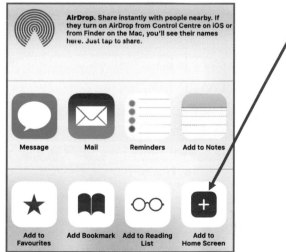

Then tap **Add** on the menu which pops up, as shown below.

This places an icon for the Facebook Web site on your Home screen, as shown in the extract below.

Windows 10

Open the Facebook full or mobile screen Web site in Web browser such as Microsoft Edge. Then tap or click the 3-dot menu button shown on the right below.

Next select **Pin this page to Start** as shown at the top of the next page.

Find on page

Print

Pin this page to Start

F12 Developer Tools

Then select **Yes** from the pop-up menu shown below.

This app is trying to pin a tile to Start   ✕

Do you want to pin this tile to Start?

Yes   No

This creates a tile for Facebook on the Windows Start screen, as shown in the extract below. Tap or click the tile to open your chosen Facebook Web site — full or mobile.

Key Points: Getting Set Up

- Facebook is a *Web site* which can easily be accessed using a free *app* from your app store.

- The app must be *downloaded* and *saved* on every device on which you want to run Facebook.

- An *icon* or a *tile* is added when you install the app, making it easy to launch Facebook.

- Facebook can also be opened in a *Web browser* such as Chrome, Safari, or Microsoft Edge.

- The *full* browser version, **www.facebook.com**, is compatible with desktops, laptops and some tablets.

- The *mobile* browser version, **m.facebook.com**, designed for smartphones and tablets, is very similar in look and feel to the app.

- The full browser version displays more features on the screen at any one time than the mobile version.

- The mobile browser version can also be used on desktops and laptops as well as phones and tablets.

- You can use the Web browser approach to run Facebook on any Internet-ready device, without having to download an app to each device.

- An icon or a tile can be added to simplify opening Facebook in a Web browser.

3

Creating Your Profile

Introduction

First of all you need to create a Facebook account. The only requirements are that you are at least 13 years of age and have a genuine e-mail address or alternatively a mobile phone number. These are needed because Facebook sends you a code by e-mail or text message. This must be typed in to confirm that you are who you say you are.

The work in this chapter is based on the Facebook app running on an Android tablet. However, the basic methods for setting up your Facebook account are the same whether you're using the Facebook app or the Web bowser approach to Facebook, as discussed in Chapter 2. Similarly the methods are essentially the same whatever device you're using — smartphone, tablet, laptop or desktop PC running Android, iOS (iPhone and iPad), or Windows operating systems.

First open Facebook by tapping the icon on your Home screen, as shown below.

Android

iOS (iPhone and iPad)

Windows 10

Creating a Facebook Account

Tap or click the Facebook icon or tile on your Home screen. The **LOG IN** screen opens, shown below for the Android Facebook app. Existing users of Facebook can sign in with their email address and password. New users should tap or click **CREATE NEW FACEBOOK ACCOUNT**.

The more traditional **Sign Up** or **Log In** screen used on the Web at **www.facebook.com** is shown below.

To create a new Facebook account, you can sign up using your **mobile number** or your **email address**, as shown on the next page. This is used when you log in or if you need to reset your password.

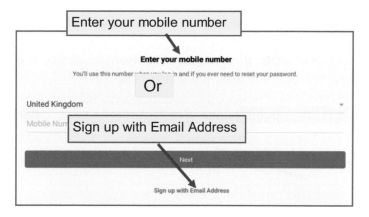

After tapping **Next** enter your first name and surname. Using your real name should ensure that your friends recognise you. Then create a password of at least 6 numbers, letters and punctuation marks.

You are asked to enter your date of birth by scrolling to select the day, month and year as shown below. (Users of Facebook must be at least 13 years of age.)

Tapping **Learn More** shown above displays a note explaining that your date of birth is used to ensure that you get a Facebook experience appropriate to your age.

To hide your birthday on your Profile/ Timeline, set the *audience selector* to **Only Me** as shown on page 43.

As a security check, a code is sent to your mobile number in a text message or in an e-mail. Enter the code into the window shown below and tap **Confirm** to show that the mobile number or e-mail address is your own

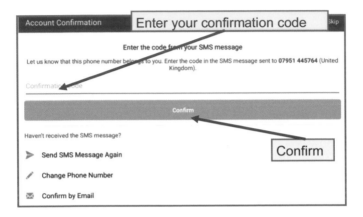

You are then asked to add a profile picture so that friends can recognise you. Either take a new photo with your smartphone, etc., or you upload one of your saved photos by selecting **Choose From Gallery**, shown below.

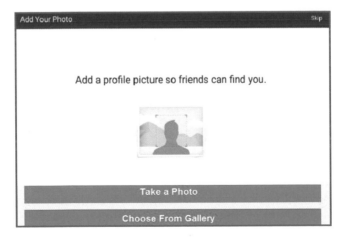

Taking a Photo

If you're using a smartphone or tablet, this option is a simple way to add your profile picture to Facebook, using the built-in camera on your device. Modern laptops also have a built-in camera. If using a desktop computer, inexpensive webcams which plug into the computer via a cable are available.

Alternatively you might want to copy an existing photo print and upload it to Facebook. Organising and managing photos on your device and uploading them to Facebook is discussed in more detail in Chapter 13

If you prefer you can tap or click **Skip** to postpone adding the profile photo - your photo and other parts of your profile can be changed and updated at any time.

Adding Friends

The Facebook screen, shown below, then appears.

Tap **GET STARTED** shown above, then you can start building up a list of Facebook friends, based on your email or phone contacts lists, as shown on the next page.

You are then presented with a list of
your contacts who are already on
Facebook and given the chance to add
them as Facebook friends, as shown
below.

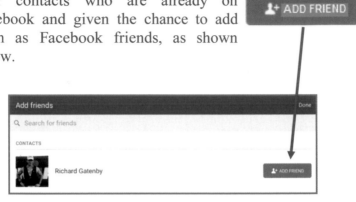

When you tap **ADD FRIEND** a friend request is sent to them,
which they can either accept or reject. A list of your
contacts who are not on Facebook is displayed with buttons
allowing you to **INVITE** them to join.

Inserting Your Photos

You're now ready to start entering your Profile. This
includes your Profile and Cover Photos and a list of details
about yourself. These might include your birthplace,
school, college, employment, etc. However, it's important
to remember that unless you select suitable privacy settings,
also known as *audience selectors*, your personal data can be
viewed by anyone.

Tap the icon shown on the right and below, then
tap your name to open your Timeline and Profile
shown on the next page.

This is your blank Profile page, ready for you to enter your Profile Photo, a Cover Photo and then enter your biographical and personal details which make up your Profile and Timeline.

Your Profile Photo is used to help people identify you. If they enter your name into a Facebook search, the result might be a long list of different people sharing the same name as you.

Adding a Profile Photo

Tap or click over the blank **Profile Photo** area on the previous page to select a photo (or video) to upload from your device to Facebook. The following menu appears.

Take a New Profile Video

Upload Video or Photo

Select Photo on Facebook

As a new user, you won't yet have any photos to allow you to use the option **Select Photo on Facebook** shown above.

Adding a Cover Photo

The Cover Photo is displayed across the top of your profile, as shown on the next page. Tap or click over the Cover Photo area shown on the previous page. This opens the menu, shown below, to select a photo saved on your device to upload to Facebook as the Cover Photo. As mentioned above, new users will not yet have any photos on Facebook itself to select from. You can adjust new photos by cropping etc., before selecting **Save** to complete the task.

Upload Photo

Select Photo on Facebook

View Cover Photo

Sample Cover and Profile photos are shown below.

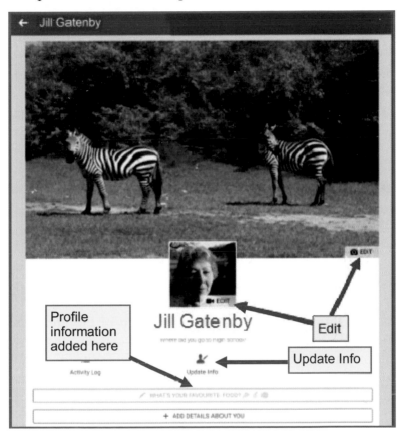

You can change your Profile Photo and Cover Photo at any time in the future by selecting **EDIT** at the bottom right-hand corner of each photo, as shown above.

Managing and transferring photos from various sources for use in Facebook (and Twitter) is discussed in more detail in Chapter 13.

Entering Your Profile Information

The Timeline, also referred to as your Profile, lists all your personal and biographical details and major events in your life, in chronological order. Obviously it's up to you to decide what to post on Facebook, which is effectively a world-wide noticeboard.

The Timeline, which includes your Profile information such as your school, college, employment, hobbies and interests is used by Facebook to identify people with similar backgrounds and interests to yourself. Then you may wish to add them to your list of Facebook friends.

You can enter your Profile information during the initial Facebook setting up process. Alternatively your Profile can be updated later e.g. if your contact details change.

If your Timeline is not open on the screen, tap the icon shown on the right. Then tap **View your Profile**.

As shown on the screenshot at the bottom of the previous page there are links asking you to enter certain pieces of information. These include your school and your favourite food. However, to see the full Profile select **ABOUT** shown below and on the screenshot on page 37.

EDIT DETAILS		
	☐ ADD FEATURED PHOTOS	
ABOUT	**PHOTOS**	**FRIENDS**

Then select **More about you** to open the Profile form as shown on the next page.

You don't have to fill in all of the information straightaway — as stated earlier, you can edit and add to your profile at any time in the future. Select **Update Info** shown on page 39 or, on some systems, **About** or **Edit Profile** on the Timeline.

What city are you from?	
WORK	
+	Add work
EDUCATION	
+	Add university
+	Add high school
PROFESSIONAL SKILLS	
+ Add your skills	
PLACES YOU'VE LIVED	
+	Add home town
+	Add current city
CONTACT INFO	
Mobile	
Facebook	
BASIC INFO	
Birthday	
Gender	

Privacy and Security

Anyone on Facebook can type your name into the Facebook search bar, find you and open your Facebook Timeline. As shown on the previous page, this can contain all sorts of important personal information, such as your employment, interests, hometown and contact details.

Facebook has built-in privacy settings known as *audience selectors* to allow you to control who can see what parts of your Profile information. You need to set these when you enter information into your Profile.

Information can be restricted to certain categories of people ranging from **Public**, (everyone can see it) through **Friends, Family** to the most restrictive **Only Me**.

Just as we need to be very careful about giving our bank and financial details to anyone else in e-mails or over the phone, then similar caution should be used with Facebook.

However, the following precautions should help to minimise the risk of crime, "scams" or unwanted or inappropriate attention on Facebook.

* Consider if it's wise to put certain information on Facebook, e.g. the days when you're away on holiday or the news that you've just won the lottery.

* Be very careful who you accept as Facebook *friends* - do you really know them and can you trust them.

* Use the audience selectors to control who can see your information, such as contact details.

Using the Audience Selectors
When Building a Your Profile

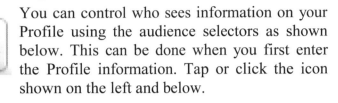

You can control who sees information on your Profile using the audience selectors as shown below. This can be done when you first enter the Profile information. Tap or click the icon shown on the left and below.

Add a subject

Attended for University ▼

⊕▼   Save Cancel

🌐 Public   ✓

👥 Friends

••• More options   ⌄

Public shown above means that anyone can see the piece of information. If you select **More options** shown above, further audiences can be selected such as **Only Me**, **Close Friends** and **Family**, as shown below.

When you've entered the data and set the required audience, select **Save** shown above.

Organising your Facebook contacts in **Lists** in addition to **Friends**, e.g. **Close Friends** and **Relations** is discussed in Chapter 4.

Editing or Updating Your Profile

After you've built up your Profile, you can edit it at anytime, including changing the audience for a particular piece of information. Open your Profile or Timeline after tapping or clicking the icon shown on the right.

Jim Gatenby
What city are you from?

:≡   👤②   ⋮
Activity Log   Update Info

| ✏ DESCRIBE WHO YOU ARE |

☎ Studied M.Phil. in Mathematical Education at University
   EDIT DETAILS

| 📷 ADD FEATURED PHOTOS |

ABOUT   **PHOTOS**   **FRIENDS**

Now select **EDIT DETAILS** or **ABOUT** shown above. On Android devices you select **ABOUT** and **More about you**.

Information which has been included in your Profile previously appears in black text with a pencil icon or a small arrow on the right. Select this icon to edit the data, including changing the audience selector.

University of Loughborough
M.Phil. in Mathematical Education

The following menu opens, including options to **Edit** or **Delete** the currently selected piece of information, in this case **school** or **university**.

⊞	See life event
✏	Edit school/university
⚙	Sharing with: Close Friends Edit privacy
⊘	Delete school/university

Selecting **Sharing with:** shown above allows you to change the audience from **Close Friends** to one of the other options such as **Public, Only Me,** and **Family** shown on page 43

Adding Information

The headings for information not yet infilled in your Profile are listed in blue such as **Add current city** on the right. Tap

or click this to add the information and set the privacy using the audience selector as shown below. Finally tap or click the **Save** button shown on page 43.

CURRENT CITY		🔽
London, United Kingdom	🌐 Public	
	👥 Friends	✓
	••• More options	⌄

Key Points: Creating Your Profile

- You can sign up to Facebook with either an e-mail address or a mobile phone number.

- Your Profile and Timeline contain biographical information about you and events in your life.

- You can take or upload a Profile Photo to help people identify you after a Facebook search.

- You don't need to enter all of your Profile information initially. Your Profile can be added to, edited and updated at any time in the future.

- Only include information in your Profile which you would be happy to post on a public noticeboard. Contact information, if included at all, should be protected with *audience selectors* discussed below.

- Some of your Profile, including your name, gender, and your photos is **Public** information, so anyone can see it, including people not on Facebook.

- Audience selectors, such as **Friends** and **Close Friends** can be used to control who sees what. *Updates* i.e. news messages, which you post on Facebook, if set as **Public**, can be seen by anyone.

Facebook Friends

Introduction

The term *friends* on Facebook covers all the people you communicate with. For example, this might include members of your family and colleagues from your work and your school days, as well as close personal friends. It may also include people with whom you share a common interest. You can invite people to be your friend and they can accept, reject or ignore the invitation.

There are various methods used by Facebook to help you find people who you might want as friends, such as:

Suggestions

From your profile information, Facebook suggests people having something in common with you, such as your home district, school, college or employer.

Search

You can enter someone's name or e-mail address into the search bar in Facebook. Then send a friend request.

Requests

You may receive requests to "friend" from someone who has seen your Profile or knows you from previous times.

Contacts

You can invite people who are in your list of email or phone contacts.

Finding Friends
Using the Facebook App

The next few pages describe the methods of finding friends using the *Facebook app* on Android and iOS (iPhone and iPad) devices. These all use similar screens and icons.

The alternative approach to accessing Facebook via a *Web browser*, as discussed in Chapter 2, uses a very different screen layout from the Facebook apps. This is described separately on page 53.

Launch Facebook from its icon on the apps screen, shown on page 31, then tap or click the three bar menu icon shown on the right. Then select **Find Friends** or **Friends** from the menu on the left-hand side, as shown below.

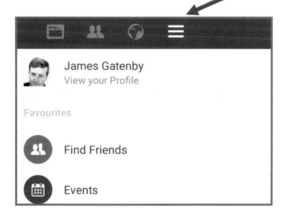

The **Find Friends** window opens, displaying buttons such as **Suggestions**, **Search**, etc., as shown on the next page.

In practice, only the currently selected button is highlighted — all of the others are greyed out, as shown on the upper screenshot on page 51, where **SEARCH** has been selected.

Suggestions

Selecting **Suggestions** shown on the top left below displays a list of people who Facebook suggests you may want as friends, based on your profile and contacts through email and mutual friends.

Requesting Someone to be Your Friend

To ask someone to be one of your Facebook friends, tap the blue **Add Friend** button against their name shown above. A request will then be sent to their Facebook account. To see any requests you've received yourself, select **Requests** shown above and on the right. The number in the red circle is the number of your new friend requests.

To find out more about a person, tap or click their name above the blue **Add Friend** button shown on the previous page. This displays their Profile, as shown below.

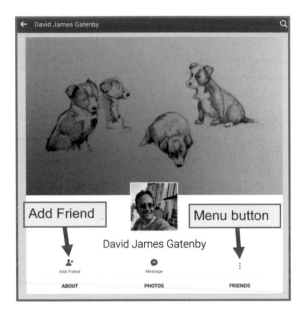

Some of the parts of your Profile, such as your Cover and Profile Photos, may have the **Public** privacy setting by default. This means anyone can see them. So someone opening a Profile from the **Suggestions** list discussed on the previous page would be able to select **ABOUT** to view the person's Profile or **PHOTOS** to see their photo albums, etc.

If, after viewing someone's Profile, you decide to "friend" them, select **Add Friend** shown on the right and on the above screenshot. This will send them a friend **REQUEST**, which they can **CONFIRM** to accept or **DELETE** to decline, as shown on page 51.

Search

The **Search** option shown below allows you to enter the name or email address of someone you would like to have as a friend on Facebook.

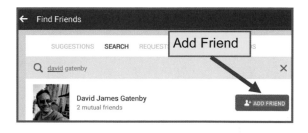

Tapping or clicking the person's name in the list of search results will open their Profile and you may be able to view their biographical details and their **Photos**, depending on their privacy settings. Then if you wish, tap or click the blue **ADD FRIEND** button shown above to send them a friend request.

Friend Requests You Receive

Select **REQUESTS** shown on page 49 to see the names of people wanting to be your Facebook friend. Then tap **CONFIRM** or **DELETE**, as shown below.

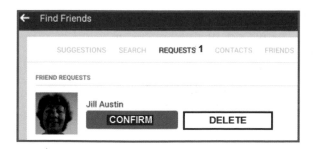

Contacts

When you select **CONTACTS** shown below, Facebook searches your lists of email and phone contacts. Anyone on the lists who is already a member of Facebook can be sent a request to be your friend.

Invitations

If there are people in your contacts lists who are not on Facebook, they can be sent an **INVITATION** to join. Tap or click the blue **INVITE** button shown below next to your contact's name to send them an invitation by email.

Finding Friends
Using a Web Browser

As discussed in Chapter 2, this is an alternative to the Facebook app and can be used on laptop and desktop computers and on the iPad and some Android tablets. The Website described here is at **www.facebook.com**, not to be confused with the *mobile* Website **m.facebook.com**, which is very similar to the Facebook app.

Open Facebook by typing **www.facebook.com** into a Web browser such as Google Chrome, Apple Safari or Microsoft Edge. Then tap or click **Find Friends** on the blue bar across the top of the screen. This opens the screen shown below.

The above screen shows the **Friend Requests** you've received, Facebook **Suggestions** for friends, finding friends from your email **Contacts** and **Search** for friends based on your Profile details. Apart from the screen layout shown above, the basic methods for finding friends are similar to those for the Facebook app discussed on pages 48-52.

Friend Lists

A major part of Facebook is the posting of *status updates* giving news and information to your friends and family, etc. These can include photos and videos, etc., and are discussed in more detail shortly. By arranging your friends into *lists*, such as **Family** and **Close Friends**, you can target your updates at specific groups of people, using *audience selectors* as discussed shortly.

So far we have looked at broad categories for the audiences who could see our information, such as **Public**, **Friends** and **Only Me** shown below.

However, we may want to refine the audiences who can see our information. For example, some people may want to communicate about work-related topics. Or you may wish to post very personal information which is only visible to your closest of friends.

Any piece of information or photograph, etc., which has the privacy set using the globe icon shown on the right, is **PUBLIC**. This means it is possible for anyone and everyone, both on and off Facebook, to see your private and personal information.

Adding Friends to a List
Using the Facebook App

From your Timeline or Profile select **FRIENDS**, then select the name of the friend you wish to include in the friend list. This opens your friend's Timeline or Profile.

Android & iPhone

On Android devices tap the icon shown on the left, which appears under your friend's Profile Photo as shown on the left below.

iPad

Open your friends Timeline or Profile as described at the top of this page. Then tap the **Friends** button shown on

the right, to the right of their Profile Photo. The following similar menus appear on the various versions of the app.

Unfollow	**Unfriend**
Unfriend	**Unfollow**
Edit Friend List	**Edit Friend Lists**
Android	**iOS (iPhone and iPad)**

Adding Friends to a List
Using a Web Browser

As mentioned earlier, this is the Web browser version of Facebook. It is also known as the *full* Website because it's designed for bigger computers than smartphones and has much more information on the screen at once. (The *mobile* Website **m.facebook.com** is designed for smartphones and is more like the Facebook apps, with much less information on the screen).

Sign in to Facebook after entering **www.facebook.com** in your browser and navigate to a friend's Timeline or Profile as before. Now select **Friends** below the Profile Photo to open the menu shown below.

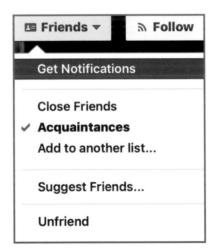

Select **Add to another list...** to add your friend with a tick to one of the existing friend lists as shown on the next page.

The options to **Unfollow** and **Unfriend** the selected friend shown on page 55 and on this page are discussed shortly.

Editing Friend Lists
Facebook App and Web Browser

This task is essentially the same whether using the app or a Web browser to access Facebook.

Tap **Edit Friend List** or **Add to another list...** shown on the previous pages to see all of your friend lists as shown below.

Edit Friend Lists	Done
★ Close Friends	✓
🔳 Acquaintances	
💼 J C Bamford Excavators Ltd	
💼 Merrill College	
💼 Rolls-Royce Group PLC	
🎓 University of Loughborough	
🏠 Family	✓
👥 Relations	✓
👤 Restricted	
♥ Good Friends	

Some of the Friend Lists such as **Family** and **Restricted** are included by default whereas others, such as your school or employment, are derived from your Profile.

Tap or click within a row to add a tick to place the selected person in the friend list such as **Family** or **Relations** as shown above. They will then receive posts which have been sent using **Family** or **Relations** as the audience.

Creating a Friend List

As shown on the previous page, a number of friend lists, such as **Good Friends** and **Close Friends**, are built into Facebook. In addition, *smart lists* are created automatically based on your Profile information such as education and work and on the communications between you and your friends.

You can also create your own friend lists, for example a cycling club called **Wheelers**. Then to post some information which is only relevant to the club members, select **Wheelers** as the *audience*. (Creating posts and selecting the audience is discussed in the next chapter).

The new list can be created using the full Facebook Web site at **www.facebook.com**. So you need to be using a tablet, laptop or desktop PC capable of running the full Web site in a *Web browser*, such as Chrome, Safari or Microsoft Edge.

Creating the List

- Launch your Web browser.
- Open the Web site **www.facebook.com**.
- Make sure the list of Facebook features is displayed down the left-hand side, if necessary by tapping the Facebook icon shown on the right, on the blue bar at the top of the screen.
- Scroll down the list on the left of the screen and hover over **FRIENDS** until **More** appears as shown below.

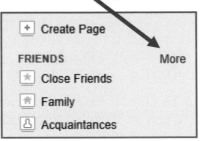

- Tap or click **More** and then select **Create List** from the **Friends** window, shown at the bottom of this page.
- Enter the name of the list, **Wheelers** in this example, and the names of the club **Members**, as shown below.

- Select the **Create** button shown above to add the **Wheelers** list to your **Friends** lists, as shown below.

So to post an update to club members only, use **Wheelers** as the audience selector, as discussed on page 87.

Acquaintances above are people you are not in regular contact with and can be excluded from posts to **Friends**.

Removing Friends or "Unfriending"
Using the Facebook App

If you no longer want to see a friend's posts on your News Feed or for them to see yours, you can *unfriend* them.

As discussed on page 55, tap or click the friend's name after selecting **FRIENDS** on your Profile or Timeline. Their Profile opens as shown in part below. For convenience the screenshots on page 55 are shown again below.

Select the **Friends** icon shown on the left and below left on your friend's Profile, then select **Unfriend** from the pop-up menu, as shown at the bottom of this page. This removes a person from your friend list and you are removed from theirs.

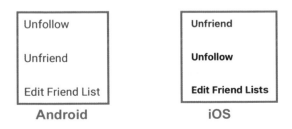

Android   iOS

Removing Friends or "Unfriending"
Using a Web Browser

On the Web site **www.facebook.com** the **Friends** and **Following** buttons appear on the right of your friend's Cover Photo, as shown below.

Tap or click **Friends** to open a menu which includes the option to **Unfriend** the selected friend, as shown at the bottom below.

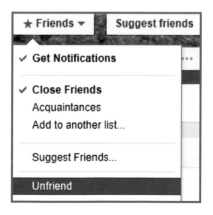

Following and Unfollowing
Using the Facebook App

A *Follower* is someone you allow to receive your Public Posts on their News Feed. By default, only Friends can follow you, unless you change your settings as discussed below.

To allow following on Android devices, from your Home Page, i.e. News Feed, tap the menu button shown above, then select **Account Settings** then **Public Posts**.

On iOS (iPhone and iPad) tap the menu button shown above, then select **Settings**, **Account Settings** then **Public Posts**.

Next tick **Public** under **Who Can Follow Me**, as shown below.

To start following someone, tap **Follow** on their Profile. If someone doesn't allow following, the **Follow** button doesn't appear on their Profile. If someone follows you they will see your posts but you won't see theirs.

A follower can **Like** your posts and **Comment** on them.

Tap or click **Unfollow** shown on page 60 to stop following someone.

Following and Unfollowing
Using a Web Browser

Tap the arrow head (normally black) on the right of the blue bar across the top of the screen, shown in white on the right below. Then select **Settings** from the menu, followed by **Public Posts** to open the window shown below.

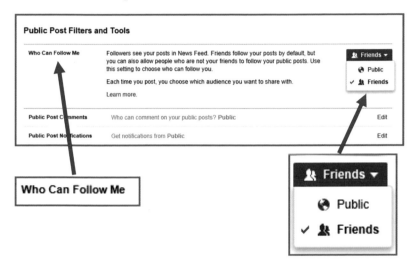

This allows you to set **Who can follow me** to either **Public** (everyone) or **Friends** as shown above. Tap **Following** on the right of the Cover Picture as shown on page 61, then to stop someone following you, select **Unfollow** from the menu.

Blocking
Facebook App and Web Browser

This stops people seeing your posts on your Timeline, inviting you to events and adding you as a friend, amongst other things. Select **Account Settings** or **Settings** then tap **Blocking**. Enter the name or e-mail address of the person then tap **Block**.

Key Points: Finding Friends

- *Friends* on Facebook are the people you share information with, not necessarily personal friends.

- Friends are *suggested* by Facebook based on your Profile or your email or phone contacts. Or you can search for friends using their name or email address.

- You can send someone a *friend request* which they can accept, reject or leave temporarily unanswered.

- Lists such as **Friends** are used as *audience selectors* to control who can see your information.

- If the **Public** setting is used it's possible, in theory, for anyone in the world to access the information.

- *Smart lists* are friend lists created automatically by Facebook, based on your exchanges with other people and on your Profile information.

- The *full Web site* **www.facebook.com** has an option to create your own friend lists.

- If you *follow* someone you can see their posts on your News Feed. You automatically follow your friends. You can also follow people who are not your friends if their privacy settings allow it.

- Facebook has options to *unfriend* and *unfollow* other users.

- *Blocking* a user stops them seeing your posts, *unfriends* them and prevents them communicating with you. You can also *unblock* blocked users.

Navigating Facebook

Introduction

This chapter shows how you can navigate around Facebook between major features such as the News Feed and your Timeline, also known as your Profile.

Many of us now use different types of computer in different situations — smartphones and tablets on the move and laptops and desktops at home or work. These different computer platforms use various *operating systems* or *user interfaces*, resulting in several versions of Facebook. As discussed in Chapter 2, the main ways to run Facebook are:

- Facebook *apps*, designed for each of the main operating systems — Android, iOS (iPhone and iPad) and Microsoft Windows 10.

- The *mobile Web site*, **m.facebook.com**, primarily designed for smartphones and tablets.

- The *full Web site*, **www.facebook.com**, used on laptop and desktop computers and on some tablets.

The above approaches to using Facebook all include the essential Facebook features and are similar in many ways. However, there are differences in the screen layouts and the ways to access certain features. This chapter is intended to help you find your way around Facebook whichever of the approaches you're using.

Signing In

Tap or click the Facebook icon on your Apps screen or, on Windows 10, tap or click the Facebook tile on the Start screen.

Alternatively, if using the Web site approach (either **m.facebook.com** or **www.facebook.com)**, open your Web browser such as Chrome, Safari or Microsoft Edge and enter the address as shown below.

Then enter your email address and password in the **Log In** window shown below.

After you tap or click **Log In**, shown above, Facebook displays your **News Feed**, also known as the **Home** page, as shown on the next page. Your News Feed displays the recent communications between you and your friends. These are known as *status updates* or *posts*.

The News Feed or Home Page

As shown below, the News Feed displays copies of the *Status Updates* posted by you and your friends. The Status Update is just a short message between friends giving latest news and sharing amusing or interesting incidents and events. The update can contain text, photos, videos and links to websites and is discussed in more detail shortly.

News Feed: Android

The News Feed is very similar on all of the mobile versions of Facebook. Shown below is the Android Facebook app with the main blue icon bar across the top of the screen.

Android App

News Feed: Mobile Web Site

The mobile Web site **m.facebook.com** is very similar in appearance to the Android Facebook app shown above and can be used on all types of device — Android, iOS (iPhone and iPad) as well as laptop and desktop PCs.

News Feed: iOS (iPhone and iPad)

The News Feed shown on page 67 is shown again below, this time displayed on an iPad. This iOS version of the Facebook app has the main icon bar at the bottom of the screen, as shown below.

iOS (iPhone and iPad) App

The Android blue icon bar on page 67 is shown again below for comparison with the iOS icon bar above.

Android

News Feed: Microsoft Windows App

Shown below is the News Feed open in the Facebook app on a Windows 10 tablet. The Windows app can also be installed and run on a laptop or desktop PC. As shown below, the Windows Facebook app displays the posts you've received down the centre.

Unlike the other Facebook apps, the Windows app normally displays the main menu down the left-hand side of the News Feed screen. The menu can be partially hidden. Clicking or tapping the menu button shown on the left below opens it.

Microsoft Windows 10 App

The panel on the right of the screen shown above shows trending news items, people you may know and may want as friends and groups you may wish to join. The **News Feed** can be selected from other screens by clicking or tapping its icon shown above. Or select **Home** also shown above.

News Feed: The Full Web Site

The Web site **www.facebook.com** used on laptop and desktop computers and on some tablets is shown below.

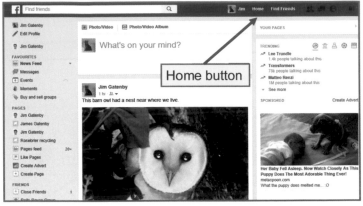

The Full Facebook Web Site

As shown above the full Web site has a blue bar across the top of the screen, displaying icons for some of the main Facebook features. The central part of the News Feed containing the updates, etc., is the same as on the Android and iOS apps and on the mobile Web site. However, the full Web site shown above, designed for bigger screens than smartphones and tablets, also displays the main menu down the left-hand side. Trending news and information is displayed in the right-hand panel shown above.

Returning to the News Feed

On mobile versions of Facebook, tap or click the icon shown on the right to return to the News Feed from any of the other Facebook screens.

On the full Web site, **www.facebook.com**, click or tap the **Home** button shown near the top of this page.

The Timeline

The News Feed or Home page, just described, shows the posts you've made and those made by your friends. The Timeline shows your Profile, biographical information, events throughout your life and the posts you've made.

As discussed earlier, when you launch Facebook and log in, your News Feed is always the start-up screen.

Opening the Timeline

Android and iOS

From the News Feed, tap the 3-bar menu button shown below.

Android   **iOS (iPhone and iPad)**

Then tap or click your name on top of the list which opens on the left-hand side of the screen, as shown below.

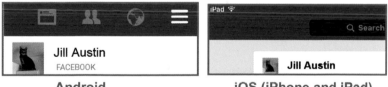

Android   **iOS (iPhone and iPad)**

Your Timeline now opens as shown on page 73.

The Facebook Mobile Web Site

Opening the Timeline from the News Feed when using the mobile Web site **m.facebook.com** is very similar to the method described above for the Android app.

Opening the Timeline

The Full Facebook Web Site

On the full Web site at **www.facebook.com**, as shown on page 70, the menu is always present on the left of News Feed page. (If using a tablet rather than a laptop or desktop computer you may need to swipe across to the right to bring the menu into view.)

So to open your Timeline from your News Feed on the full Web site, it's simply a case of tapping or clicking your name on the top of the menu, as shown below.

The Full Facebook Web Site

After selecting your name, your Timeline opens as shown on pages 73 and 74.

Windows 10

Tap or click your name or Profile Picture on the top right of the News Feed, as shown on the right and on page 69. This opens your Timeline, as shown on pages 73 and 74.

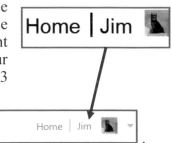

Viewing the Timelines of Friends

Selecting **FRIENDS**, shown in my Profile on page 74, lists my friends as shown below.

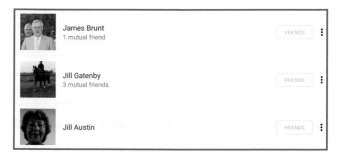

Then tap or click your friend's name as shown above to open their Timeline as shown below.

People Who are Not Your Friends

You can also view the Timelines of people who are on Facebook, but who are not your friends, after entering their name in the Facebook search bar. How much you see depends on the *audience selector* settings used in the creation of the Timeline, discussed elsewhere in this book.

Timeline Features

The Timeline features on the next few pages are similar on all the versions of Facebook — Android, iOS and Windows 10 apps and the mobile and full Web sites.

The Facebook Timeline

EDIT DETAILS on page 74 allows you to change biographical information such as your job, marital status or current city, etc. You can also write a few words about yourself after selecting **DESCRIBE WHO YOU ARE**. The **Activity Log** lists what you've been doing such as updating your photos or stories you've commented on.

Selecting **ABOUT** on the previous page lists your Profile and contact information, also your friends, with options to remove them.

Select **PHOTOS** at the bottom of page 74 to show the images you've uploaded to Facebook.

Tapping or clicking **FRIENDS** shown at the bottom of page 74 produces a list of your friends as shown on page 73.

Returning to Your News Feed

iOS (iPhone and iPad)

To return to your News Feed from the Timeline, tap or click the News feed icon shown on the right, which appears at the bottom left of the News Feed Timeline.

Android

Tap or click the arrow at the top left-hand corner of the screen, as shown on the right and on page 73. This returns you to the main menu, partly shown below. Then tap or click the News Feed icon below. The icon is greyed out on the blue menu bar prior to selection.

The Facebook Mobile Web Site

The mobile Web site **m.facebook.com** displays the News Feed icon on a blue bar at the top of the Timeline, very similar to the Android app shown above. Tap this to return to your News Feed from the Timeline.

Windows

Tap or click either **Home** or **News Feed** as shown below and on page 69.

Returning to Your News Feed

The Full Facebook Web Site

On the full Web site at **www.facebook.com**, tap or click **Home** on the blue bar shown across the top of the screen. This returns you to the News Feed from the Timeline.

To go back to the Timeline tap your name or Profile Picture in the blue bar shown above. This is an alternative to tapping or clicking your name in the menu list as described on page 72.

Logging Out of Facebook

If you're sharing a machine with other people you might want to log out of your Facebook account at the end of each session. You will then need to sign in again with your email address and password at the start of each session in the future.

Logging Out

Android

From the News Feed, select the 3-bar menu button and then select **Log Out** from the bottom of the main menu which appears down the left-hand side of the screen, as shown in part below.

From the Timeline tap or click the small arrow at the top left-hand corner of the screen to display the main menu. Then select **Log Out** from the bottom of the menu.

Mobile Web Site m.facebook.com

The method is similar to that shown above. The menu button on the right of the blue bar opens the main menu down the left-hand side of the screen, from both the News Feed and the Timeline.

Logging Out

iOS (iPhone and iPad)

From either the News Feed or the Timeline, tap the small arrow on the top right of the screen, shown below. Then select **Log Out** from the drop-down menu.

> Jim ∨
>
> **Activity Log**
>
> **Privacy Shortcuts**
>
> **Settings**
>
> **Log Out**

Windows and the Full Web Site www.facebook.com

Similar to the method shown above, an arrowhead icon on the top right of the screen is used to open a small menu which includes the option to **Log Out** of Facebook. This icon is present on both the News Feed and the Timeline. On the full Web site the arrowhead icon is initially black but changes to white when selected, as shown on the right.

> Activity Log
>
> News Feed Preferences
>
> Settings
>
> Log out

Key Points: Navigating Facebook

- Facebook can be accessed using the *apps* for Android, iOS and Windows 10 devices or by either the mobile or the full Facebook Web site. After you sign in to Facebook, the *News Feed* or *Home Page* opens showing the latest posts from your friends.

- You can switch to your Timeline/Profile by selecting the menu button shown on the right and then selecting your name on the menu on the left of the screen.

- You can switch back to the News Feed from the Timeline using the News Feed icon. Or select **Home** on the blue bar, where available.

- The Android and iOS apps and the mobile Web site display the News Feed and Timeline on uncluttered, separate screens.

- The Windows Facebook app and the full Web site display menus and other features simultaneously on the News Feed screen.

- You can view the Timeline, Profile and photos, of friends and also people who are not your friends, as far as their privacy settings allow.

- A drop-down menu allows you to **Log Out**. Your password must be entered next time you (or anyone else) wants to view or edit your Facebook or post updates.

Posting Facebook Updates

Introduction

Previous chapters attempted to show the sort of things you can do with Facebook and how to get started. Also the different approaches, i.e. using one of the Facebook *apps* or opening either the full or mobile Facebook Web site in a *Web browser* such as Google Chrome, Safari, etc.

It was also necessary early on to describe the making of *friends* on Facebook, essential for any worthwhile use of the social network. Similarly to describe the creation of your Profile and Timeline, which are used to find and suggest potential friends from people having similar backgrounds and interests to yourself.

It was also felt important to cover the ways of controlling the audience for your Facebook posts and your Profile, to protect your *privacy* and *security*. This chapter covers the main day to-day activities of using Facebook, such as:

- Posting an *Update* from your News Feed and Timeline. Posting to a friend's Timeline.

- Including a photo, video, Web link, location, activities, emoticons and who you're with.

- Selecting the *audience* for the update.

- Responding to an update. **Like**, **Comment**, **Share**.

- Using Facebook Live to *broadcast* or *stream* live video to a selected audience.

Posting a Status Update

The Status Update is used to tell other people your latest news, where you are and what you're doing and to share photos and videos. These notes apply to all of the devices and approaches used to access Facebook.

Posting an Update from the Timeline

Tap or click **Status** or **What's on your mind?** on the Timeline, as shown below, to open the **Update status** window shown on the next page.

Posting an Update from the News Feed

From the News Feed as shown below, tap or click **What's on your mind?** (Or select **Status** on some systems).

The **Update status** window opens as shown below. Yo
can start typing after tapping or clicking **What's on your
mind?** On mobile devices the on-screen keyboard pops up.

Although many updates are very brief news
items, an update can actually be up to 63,206
characters long.

Select any of the icons shown on the
right and on the centre right above to
add photos and other features to the
post, as discussed on the next page.

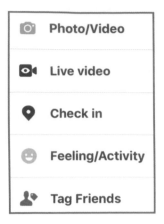

Photo/Video

Select from the media stored on your device a photo or video to include in your update.

Live video

Record and share a video. Can be used to broadcast, i.e. stream a live video to a selected audience. Discussed in more detail later in this chapter.

Check in

Display a list of nearby businesses and restaurants, etc. Select one to add your current location to the update.

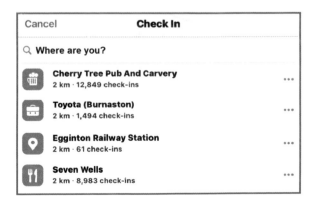

Feeling/Activity

This option offers a choice of activities and icons to say what you're doing and how you're feeling.

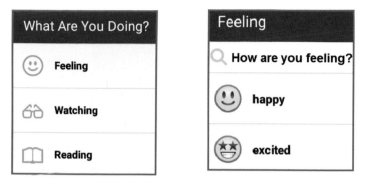

Listed above on the left are a few of the many feelings and activities for you to choose from. Select **Feeling** to display a huge range of *emoticons* such as **happy** and **excited** shown in the sample on the right above.

There are many more activities listed on the screen, in addition to **Feeling**, **Watching** and **Reading** shown above. For example, **Travelling to** displays a list of worldwide destinations so you can tell friends where you're going to, as shown in the small sample below.

Tag Friends

This presents a list of your Facebook friends so you can include in your update the names of any who are currently with you.

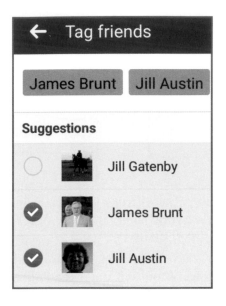

The details you select, as just described, such as your current location, what you're doing and who you're with, are automatically added to the top of the update, as shown below. The cake icon shown below was inserted after selecting the **Feeling/Activity** icon shown on pages 83 and 84 and then choosing the **Celebrating** category.

 James Gatenby 🎂 celebrating a birthday with **Jill Austin** at ⚲ **Cherry Tree Pub And Carvery.**
Yesterday at 10:50 · 👥

Selecting the Audience

To control who will share your update, select **Friends** below your name, then choose the audience as shown below, such as **Public** (anyone can see the update) and **Friends**, also shown below. Select **More** ... to see further options. Finally select **Done**.

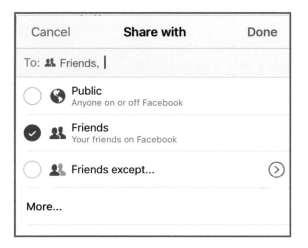

Posting

When the update is complete with your text, any pictures, location, companions, etc., select **POST** shown on the right and on page 83. The update will very quickly appear on your Timeline and News Feed and on the News Feeds of your friends, according to the audience selected in the **Share with** window as shown above. As discussed on page 91, you can also post an update to the Timeline of a selected friend.

Receiving an Update

When you post an update, a copy appears in your News Feed and on your Timeline. The update also appears on the News Feeds of the people in your selected audience, such as **Friends**, as shown on page 87.

You can respond to an update after tapping or clicking the **Like**, **Comment** and **Share** buttons shown above and described on the next page.

Responding to an Update

Like

Tap or click the thumbs up sign if you **Like** the update. After someone likes an update the thumbs up sign appears again in a blue circle as shown below. Tap or click this to see a list of people who have already liked the update.

You, Jill Austin and 14.9K others   95 comments 31.2K shares

👍 Like   💬 Comment   ➡ Share

You can also choose from a selection of emoticons to express how you feel about the update.

Comment

Selecting **Comment** above opens a small window in which you can write a response to the post. You can also select **comments** above to see what other people have written.

Share

Share allows you to post the update to your friends, write a post or send in *Facebook Messenger*. Messenger is discussed in Chapter 7.

↻ **Share Now (Friends)**

☑ **Write Post**

● **Send in Mesenger**

➡ **Share**

sting a Web Link in a Status Update

you think your friends may be interested in a particular
Web site, you can send a live *link* or *hyperlink* as part of a
status update. Tap or click **What's on Your Mind?** (or **Status**
on some systems) in your Timeline or News Feed to open
the **Update Status** window shown below. Then enter the
address of the Web site you wish to share, together with a
message, as shown below.

Use the audience selector to control who will see the post,
as discussed on page 87. Then tap the **Post** button shown
above and the live Web site link soon appears in blue on
the News Feeds of your friends.

Friends can then tap the link to open the website, in this
example **www.babanibooks.com**, in their Web browser,
such as Google Chrome, Apple Safari or Microsoft Edge.

Posting to a Friend's Timeline

Normally when you post an update with **Friends** as the audience, it will appear in their News Feeds. However, you might want to post an update to just a particular friend. This can be done by posting to their Timeline.

From your own Timeline select **Friends** and then tap the name of your friend in the list which appears. This opens the friend's Timeline as shown below.

In the above example, I have opened Jill's Timeline from my own Timeline by selecting her name in my **Friends** list.

Next tap or click **Write Post** or **Share Photo** on your friend's Timeline and write the text and insert any pictures, etc., as described from pages 83 onwards. Then tap the **Post** button and the update will soon appear on your friend's Timeline.

To control who can post on your Timeline, etc., select the 3-bar menu button, then **Account Settings** or **Settings/Account Settings** followed by **Timeline and Tagging** as discussed on pages 117 and 118. Then set your required audience as discussed on page 87.

acebook Live

This feature allows you to share a live video with an audience which you select, as discussed on page 87. Unlike the *video call* discussed in Chapter 7, Facebook Live streams or broadcasts your video to everyone in the audience. In the video call you see each other's videos. Facebook Live is used by public figures such as musicians, actors and celebrities to broadcast to all their followers, as well as private individuals sharing a video with friends. Your audience could be set at **Public** so that anyone on Facebook can see the video. Or to practise with Facebook Live, you could select **Only Me** before extending it to a wider audience, such as **Friends**.

Tap **What's on your mind?** from your News Feed, as shown on page 82. Then select **Live video** or **Go Live** from the menu which appears.

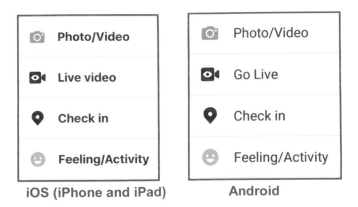

iOS (iPhone and iPad)　　Android

The video screen opens as shown on the next page. This allows you to select your intended audience as shown on page 87, type a few words to **Describe your live video...** and select either front or rear facing cameras.

To start the streaming the video to your audience, tap the blue **Go Live** button shown above. After counting down from 3, the video starts. While streaming is in progress a red live button is displayed on the screen. Your friends are notified if you are broadcasting so they can join in. The video can be streamed for up to 90 minutes.

Finally tap or click **FINISH**. You can then select either to **Delete** or **Post** the video. The posted video is saved in your Timeline and News Feed and your friends' News Feeds.

Facebook Mentions is similar to Facebook Live and is a separate app intended only for *verified public figures* such as celebrities, musicians, actors, athletes, etc., to broadcast to their fans and supporters.

Key Points: Posting Facebook Updates

- An *update* or *status update* is a news message and may include photos and videos as well as text up to a limit of 63,206 characters.

- Buttons or screen icons allow you to select and include in the update your current location, activities, companions and feelings, expressed in the form of *emoticons* such as a smiley face.

- An update can be posted from your News Feed (also known as your Home page) or your Timeline.

- A copy of your update appears on the News Feeds of the people in the audience which you selected.

- You can post an update on a friend's Timeline after selecting them in the **Friends** list on your Timeline.

- Anyone receiving an update can **Like** it, add a **Comment** or **Share** it with friends, etc.

- You can list the names and comments of other people who've received and liked the same update.

- The **Timeline and Tagging** option in the **Account Settings** menu allows you to control access to your Timeline.

- *Facebook Live* is used to broadcast, i.e. stream, live video to a selected audience such as **Friends** or **Public**. *Facebook Mentions* is a broadcasting app used by public figures, celebrities, etc.

Facebook Messenger

Introduction

Facebook Messenger (also referred to more simply as Messenger) is a new, separate app which, amongst other things, has taken over the chat and text messaging features previously built into the main Facebook app. The Messenger activities discussed in this chapter, are:

- Exchanging *text messages* with friends, including *Chatting* with friends who are currently online, exchanging text messages in *real time*.

- *Recording voice* messages which are included with a play button along with the text messages.

- Including your own *photos, videos* and *location* information and a map within the message.

- Taking photos and making videos with the camera on your device.

- Inserting cartoon icons and short video clips to add humour and express feelings in messages.

- Making *voice* and *video calls* to anywhere in the world, free of charge when using Wi-Fi.

Permissions

In order to use all of the full Messenger features you need to have a microphone and camera on your device. These are normally built into smartphones, tablets and laptops but you may need to buy a separate webcam and microphone for a desktop PC.

Messenger

You may need to give Messenger permission to access your camera and microphone. This may be requested when you first start using Messenger. Otherwise you can switch the permissions on in your device settings as discussed below.

Android

- Swipe down twice from the top and tap the gear wheel **Settings** icon, shown on the right.

- Select **Apps**, scroll down and select **Messenger**.

- Select **Permissions**.

- Make sure **Camera**, **Location** and **Microphone** are all **ON**.

iOS (iPhone and iPad) and Windows

- Select the **Settings** icon from the iOS Apps screen or the Windows Start menu.

  iOS   Windows

- Select **Privacy**.

- Make sure **Location** or (**Location Services**) is **ON** and **Microphone** and **Camera** are both **ON**.

Sound

You may also need to switch the in-applications sound **ON** on your device. This is found within **Settings** on Android, in **Facebook Settings** on iOS devices and in the **Control Panel** in Windows.

Installing Messenger

The Messenger app is free to install from the app store for your particular device — Android, iOS (iPhone and iPad) or Microsoft Windows. After you've installed Messenger, the first time you open it you can choose how to sign up. Either use the e-mail address and password from an existing Facebook account, or enter a phone number which friends can use to chat or send messages to you. (Messenger can be used by someone without a Facebook account).

Using Messenger

On Android and iOS devices, Messenger is launched by tapping its icon on the app screen as shown below.

Android   **iOS (iPhone and iPad)**

On Microsoft Windows, the Messenger app appears in the list of apps on the Start Menu on the left of the screen, as shown on the left below.

Windows

To place a *tile* for Messenger on the Windows Start menu, right-click or tap and hold the Messenger icon or name shown on the left above. Then click or tap the **Pin to Start** button which appears, as shown on the right above.

Messenger opens, displaying the Home screen shown below on an Android tablet. (Other devices such as iOS smartphones and tablets may use different screen colours and layouts but the icons and their functions are basically the same).

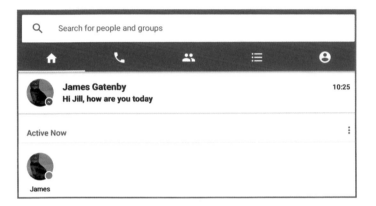

The screen above is from Jill's Messenger account and includes a message from James. If Jill taps or click this message, the main message window opens showing all of the messages or chats between Jim and Jill. Space at the bottom is provided for Jill to **Write a message** before selecting the **Send** icon shown on the right and below.

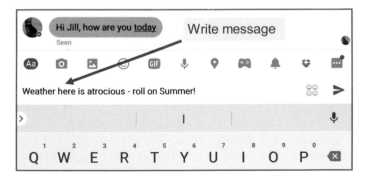

Jill and James are both online to Messenger simultaneously, so a real-time Chat, i.e. conversation or exchange of text messages can take place, with each person giving an immediate response to the other's message.

The messages you've sent appear against a blue background on your device. Messages you receive have a grey background and show the sender's Profile Photo.

Friends Who Have Messenger

When you sign in to Messenger, your contacts are listed on the Home screen. Small circular icons at the bottom right of the Profile Pictures, as shown below, indicate whether or not a friend uses Messenger and if they are currently **Active**, i.e. logged on to Messenger.

Doesn't have Messenger

Uses Messenger

Logged on to Messenger

Writing a New Message

Open Messenger by tapping or clicking its icon, as shown on the right. Then select the appropriate new message icon as shown below.

Messenger

Android   **iOS**   **Windows**

On Android devices you can choose to make either a phone call or write, i.e. type, a text message.

Next, on all devices, select the intended recipient of the message from the list which appears.

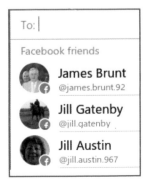

Any previous conversations you've had with your contact will be appear as shown on page 99. Otherwise the top of the screen will be blank. If your contact is not already a user of Messenger, they are sent an invitation including a link to install the Messenger app.

Tap or click **Type a message** or **Write a message...** shown below to display the on-screen keyboard (on mobile devices) and then begin typing the message.

As shown below, there is a large set of icons at the bottom of the screen. Similar icons appear on the different devices — Android, iOS and Windows.

These icons allow you to add a range of additional features and information to the text of your message as discussed on the next page.

If you run Messenger on a machine lacking certain equipment, a more limited set of icons is displayed. For example, on a Windows PC with no camera, the camera icon shown above will not appear. You must also give Messenger permission to use a camera and microphone, as discussed earlier in this chapter.

The Messenger Icons

Some or all of the icons shown below will be displayed on the screen while you're typing a message. Most of them allow you to insert extra features in addition to the basic text of the message.

 Return from another screen to the message typing window, ready to continue typing.

 Use the camera on your device to take a photo or video to be included in the message. Initially you may be asked to give Messenger permission to access your camera.

 Include a photo or video clip which is already stored on the camera roll of your device.

 Choose a *sticker*, as shown below, to add to message. There a many stickers to choose from in different categories. These are colourful images, as shown below and some of them are animated.

GIFS are special files containing very short videos which keep repeating themselves. These might be seasonal greetings such as a New Year message, a firework display or an amusing clip.

 Send a voice message to your friend. Useful if you don't want to type a long message. Tap or click and hold the red button which appears, then release to end the recording. The recording appears in the message with a play button and the duration in seconds as shown below.

This lets you select from a list of nearby places, to tell your friend where you are. The *location* or place name, such as a hotel, is inserted into the message, and the place also pinpointed on a map of the area.

Include this icon in a conversation to show that you **Like** it.

Sending a Message

When you've finished typing the message and inserted any of the extra features described on the previous pages, tap the **Send** icon shown on the right.

If your friend is currently signed in to Messenger they will receive your message and any photos, etc., straightaway. You can then start an online conversation or Chat.

When you send a message, a white tick in a solid blue circle indicates the message has been delivered to your friend's Messenger account, as shown below.

> When shall we meet up Jill?

After your friend has read the message their Profile Picture replaces the ticked circle, as shown below.

> When shall we meet up Jill?

Chat Heads

If your friend is using an app other than Messenger when you send a message, a *Chat Head*, based on your Profile Picture, appears on their current screen. Tap or click the Chat Head to open Messenger and start a Chat.

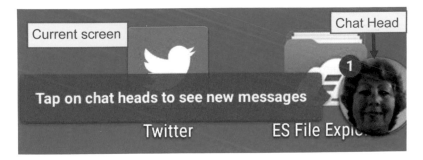

A Conversation

Shown below is a live Chat, where both friends are online, so comments can be exchanged, like a telephone call only with typed Instant Messages, often referred to as **IM**s.

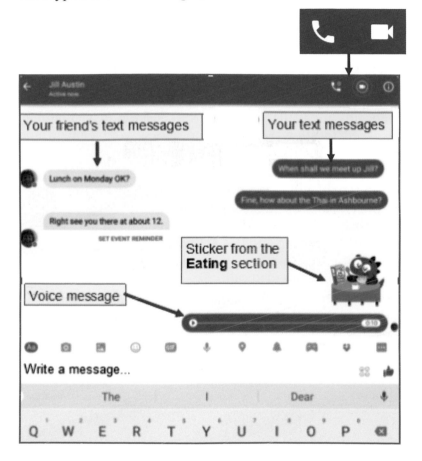

Also shown above is a 10 second recorded voice message, and a Sticker, a colourful or amusing image selected from a library as discussed earlier in this chapter.

Voice and Video Calls

A video call lets you see and hear the person you are talking to. You can make *free* voice and video calls to someone anywhere in the world, if using a Wi-Fi network. These are now available in many public places such as libraries, coffee bars, hotels, trains, buses and airports. If using a 3G/4G mobile phone network for your Internet connection, a charge may be deducted from your data plan.

Smartphones, tablets and laptops generally have a camera and microphone built in. Separate microphones and Webcams are available to plug into desktop PCs. You may be asked to allow Messenger to access your camera and microphone the first time you try to use them.

Making a Call

If you're already involved in an online text chat with a friend, icons at the top right of the conversation as shown on the right and on the previous page allow you to start a voice or video call.

Alternatively, with the **Home** screen selected as shown in blue below, tap the **Calls** icon, also shown below.

Home   Calls   Groups   People   Me

A list of names appears with icons for voice and video calls against their name. The green dot indicates they are online and available to answer your call.

If the person you call is online they can select either the green button to accept it or red to reject it, as shown the right. If they are not online to the Internet, you are given the chance to record a voice message. They are notified of your call next time they're online.

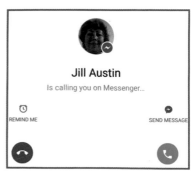

Receiving Voice Calls

If you accept a voice-only call, the following screen allowing you to switch video on if you wish, as shown on the right.

Other icons allow you to mute the microphone, switch off the speaker (where possible) and end the call.

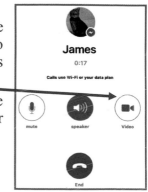

Receiving Video Calls

If you accept a video call, the icons shown below appear at the bottom of the screen. If you have a smartphone or tablet with both front and rear facing cameras you can either display yourself in a "selfie" or show a video of your surroundings, etc. Use the camera icon shown on the right and below to switch between font and rear facing cameras.

Key Points: Facebook Messenger

- You can sign up to Messenger using your Facebook account details, or just using a phone number.

- Send text messages to friends currently off-line. Chat with friends currently online, in a two-way, real-time exchange of text messages.

- Record *voice messages* if you don't have time to type a long message.

- Take photos and make videos to include with the message. Include in the message photos and videos stored in the gallery on your device.

- Choose from thousands of *stickers* or *emoticons* such as smiling faces, to include in the message to express how you feel.

- View your conversations, i.e. lists of exchanges, with a friend, in a window on your device. Icons show when your message has been viewed by your friends.

- Make and receive *live voice* and *video* phone calls with friends and family anywhere in the world.

- Calls can be made between devices with different operating systems, such as Android and iOS (iPhone and iPad).

- Calls are free when you're connected to Wi-Fi, otherwise if using a mobile phone network you are charged according to your data plan.

8

Reviewing Your Privacy

Introduction

Chapter 3 showed how you can use the *audience selectors* to set the level of privacy on individual parts of your Profile. Chapter 4 discussed how it's possible, depending on your privacy settings, for complete strangers to see your Profile after entering your name in a search on Facebook.

You may not want the whole world to be able to see your personal and financial information, contact details and family photos, etc. So to keep your personal information private you need to use audience selectors such as **Friends**, etc., as discussed in Chapters 3 and 4. In addition to **Friends**, you can also create your own *Friend Lists*, as discussed in Chapter 4, for different categories of audience. Here the word "friends" is used loosely, as some lists may include people who are not personal friends but who you need to communicate with through your work, etc.

Facebook sets some privacy settings by default. For example, when you create a new post or status update as discussed in Chapter 6, the privacy is set at **Friends**. However, some other information such as parts of your Profile, may be set at **Public**.

This chapter shows how you can carry out a comprehensive review of your privacy settings and change them if necessary.

Privacy Shortcuts

This feature allows you to review your privacy settings and change them if necessary. The method of opening the shortcuts is slightly different for the various apps and the full Facebook Web site, as shown below.

Android and iPhone

Tap the 3-dot menu button shown on the right and in its location on the Profile shown on page 60. Then select **View Privacy Shortcuts** from the menu which appears. The iPhone uses a similar but horizontal menu button on the right of the Profile screen.

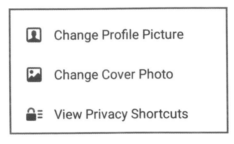

iPad

Tap the arrow head on the right of the blue bar at the top of the screen. Then select **Privacy Shortcuts** as shown below.

Facebook Website www.facebook.com

Click or tap the padlock icon on the right of the blue bar across the top of the screen, as shown on the right. The **Privacy Shortcuts** menu opens, as shown in part below.

All Versions of Facebook

Whichever of the approaches to Facebook you are using, you can now see the **Privacy Shortcuts** menu with the options shown below.

Privacy Check-up

Select **Privacy Check-up**, as shown on the previous page. Select **CONTINUE** to check the privacy settings on three main parts of Facebook. These are your **Posts**, your **Profile** and the **Apps** you've used Facebook to log into.

Posts

This guides you through your current audience settings for the next post from your News Feed or your Profile.

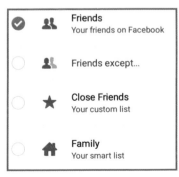

```
←  Posts                                          Next

                    ●─○─○

      Whenever you post from News Feed or your Profile, you can
              choose an audience to control who sees it.


Your next post

Choose Audience                                 ⅈ Friends ▾


Tip: You can change your audience each time you post.
```

To change the audience from **Friends**, tap or click the arrow next to **Friends** shown above, then select **More...** to see the available additional audiences shown in part below.

Friends
Your friends on Facebook

Friends except...

Close Friends
Your custom list

Family
Your smart list

Profile

After tapping or clicking **Next** your Profile is displayed showing all your current privacy settings, which again can be changed if you wish, as discussed on page 112.

iPad 🔋	11:30	✈ ⅄ 96% ▮▮
Back	**Profile**	Next

◉—●—○

Have a look at this info from your Profile and decide who to share it with. Remember, your Profile may include more than what's here.

PHONE

07583704218	🔒 Only Me ▾

EMAIL

jimgatenby@tesco.com	👥 Friends ▾

BIRTHDAY

2 March	👥 Friends ▾
1899	🔒 Only Me ▾

WORK

Rolls-Royce Group PLC Engine Performance	📍 Derby Area ▾
J C Bamford Excavators Ltd Technical Author	👥 Friends ▾
Merrill College Head of Computing and Mathematics Teacher	👥 Friends ▾

These are your own default settings which will apply if you take no further action. However, you can, if you wish, change individual settings at any time in the future.

Apps

After selecting **Next** you are able to select the audience who sees the apps that you've used Facebook to log in to and delete any you no longer want.

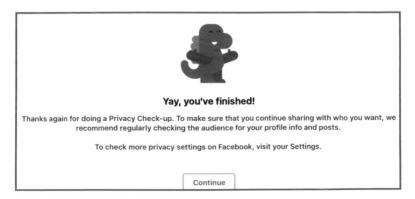

Finally select **Done**, or **Next** followed by **Close** to complete the **Privacy Check-up**. You are then advised by Facebook to regularly check the audience for your posts and Profile.

Who can see my stuff?

From the **Privacy Shortcuts** menu shown on page 111, select **Who can see my stuff?** to open the settings shown below.

Selecting **Who can see your future posts?** displays a list of all of your possible audiences ranging from **Public** through **Friends** to **Relations** and audiences based on your Profile information.

Selecting the lower option on the previous page **Where do I review who can see things I've posted or been tagged in** opens your **Activity Log**. This presents a list of months which, when selected, display the posts you've sent, etc.

The next heading on page 111 **Who can contact me?** allows you to select who can send you friend requests.

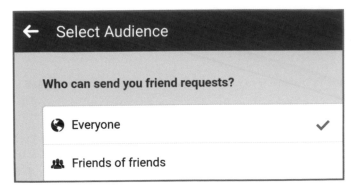

How do I stop someone from bothering me? shown on page 111 opens the blocking option shown below.

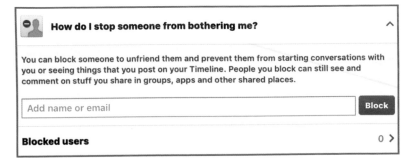

Enter a person's name or email address and tap or click **Block** to unfriend them and stop them seeing your posts as discussed on page 61. Tap or click **Blocked users** shown above, to display a list of people you've already blocked.

Further Privacy Settings
Android

On Android devices, tapping the menu icon shown on the right, on the blue bar across the top of the screen. Scroll down and select **Account Settings** then select **Privacy** shown below.

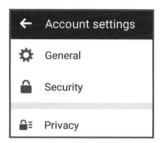

This opens the **How you connect** window shown on page 119.

iOS (iPhone and iPad)

Tap the 3-bar menu button shown on the right, on the bar along the bottom of the screen. Then scroll down and select **Settings** and **Account Settings** shown below.

Next select **Privacy** shown below to open the **How you connect** window shown on page 119.

Settings

🌐 **General**

🛡️ **Security**

🔒 **Privacy**

▯ **Timeline and Tagging**

www.facebook.com

With the full Facebook Web site open at **www.facebook.com** tap or click the black arrowhead icon on the blue bar at the top of the screen As shown on the right, this changes to white when selected.

Jim   Home   Find Friends

Then select **Settings** and **Privacy** from the drop-down menu. This opens a screen with similar privacy settings to those shown in the **How you connect** window on page 119.

The default setting **Everyone** shown in the **How you connect** window on page 119 gives no protection against anyone wanting to access your information on Facebook.

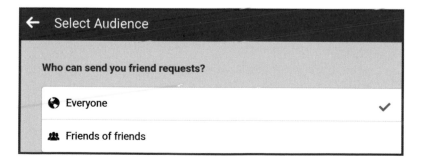

To change a privacy setting, tap or click anywhere in a row to select with a tick the new audience such as **Friends of friends** from the menu that appears, as shown below.

Key Points: Reviewing Your Privacy

- The **Privacy Check-up** feature in **Privacy Shortcuts** lists your current privacy settings for the posts made from your Profile or from your News Feed. This is set at **Friends** by default but you can change it in the **Check-up** if you wish. You can also change the audience each time you create an individual post.

- The **Privacy Check-up** also allows you to review who can see the information in your Profile such as your contact details, etc., and change the audiences if necessary.

- If you use Facebook to log in to other *apps*, you can control who sees which apps you've been using.

- You can control who can send you *friend requests* and who can see posts you've been mentioned or *tagged* in. (Tagging is discussed in Chapter 6).

- As shown in the **How you connect** window on page 119, some of the settings are set at **Everyone** by default. You may wish to consider changing some of these settings.

- By default, *search engines* outside of Facebook, e.g. Google, are allowed to access your Profile. You may wish to prevent this by changing **Yes** to **No** in the section **Who can look me up?** in **How you connect** shown on page 119.

More Facebook Features

Introduction

Previous chapters have covered the basic skills needed to get started with Facebook and how to use the main features. These include your Profile or Timeline, News Feed, Facebook Friends, and involve communication in various forms such as status updates including photos and videos. Also text messages and chats, live voice and video calls and videos broadcast or streamed to a selected audience.

With these basic skills you should now be able to explore some other useful features on Facebook such as those listed below and briefly described in the rest of this chapter.

- *Facebook Apps*: software such as games and utilities for uploading photos, etc.

- *Groups*: Getting together online with other people to share information about a common interest.

- *Notifications*: Notes generated by Facebook informing you that something has happened on Facebook involving you.

- The *Poke*: Letting people know you're active on Facebook.

- *Events*: Publicising forthcoming events with the place, date and time.

- *Facebook Pages*: special pages designed to promote a business, organisation, celebrity or cause.

Facebook Apps and Games

These are applications, i.e. programs, which work within the Facebook environment. Some Apps are provided for free by Facebook itself while others are sold by third-party developers.

Open the menu on the left-hand side of the Facebook Home page, using the icon shown on the right. On Android devices scroll down and select **Instant Games**, to open the window partly shown below.

Alternatively, type the name of an app into the search bar at the top of the window.

On iOS (iPhone and iPad) devices select **Apps** from the menu on the Home screen, then select **Games**.

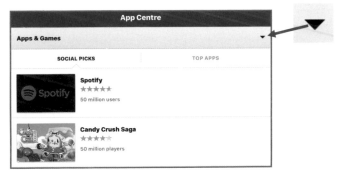

Tap the arrow at the top right of the screen then select **Apps & Games** to see more apps in the Facebook **App Centre**.

Facebook Groups

A Group on Facebook is a page shared by a number of people with a common interest. You can join a group you're interested in or create a new group of your own. A group can have just a few members or several thousand.

For example, you might want to find out about any groups already up and running on a particular subject or hobby such as cycling. Enter **cycling** into the Facebook search bar and then select **Groups**. A long list of groups is displayed.

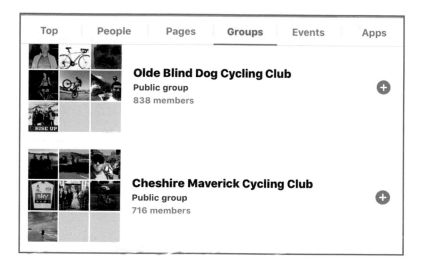

To find out about a particular group, tap or click its name as shown above. The Facebook page for the group opens as shown on the next page. In this example, the cycling club Home page states the aims of the group. Typical members' posts on the Facebook group might include discussions about fitness, invitations to friends to join a forthcoming ride, or buying and selling spare cycle parts. Select the button shown on the right and above to send a request to become a member of a group.

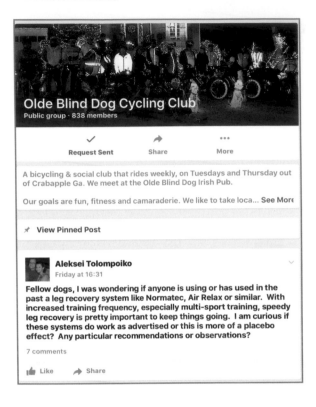

Creating a Group

From the menu on the left-hand side of your Home page, on Android and Windows select **Groups**, followed by **CREATE** then **CREATE GROUP**. On iOS (iPhone and iPad) select Groups then tap the **+** sign, as shown below.

Then select a goal for the group as shown on the next page.

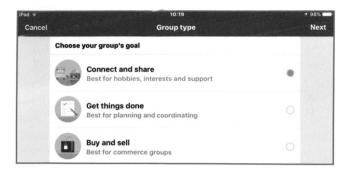

Now tap or click **Next** and enter a name for the group and the names of the people you want to be members. Then tap or click **Next** and select the privacy for the group from **Public**, **Closed** or **Secret** and finally select **Create** to complete the process.

Notifications

These are messages, informing you of activity on Facebook that involves you or your friends.

Check your **Notifications** by tapping or clicking the icon shown below.

The Poke

This is a quick way to say hello to someone and to let them know you exist and are still on Facebook. Tap the 3-bar menu button shown on the right. Then scroll down the menu and select **Apps** and then **Pokes**. On Android you may need to select **See all** under **Apps** and then select **Pokes**. Then enter the name of the friend in the Search bar and tap **Yes**, as shown below. Facebook also suggests a number of friends you may wish to poke.

← Pokes 🔍

Poke Jill Austin?

| Yes | No |

An alternative approach to Poke a friend is to select the 3-dot menu button on the right of their Profile/Timeline then select **Poke**.

After you poke your friend, they receive a notification and are given the chance to **Poke back** as shown below.

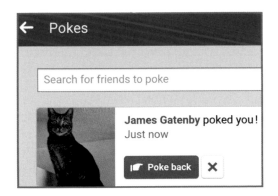

Events

This feature allows you to publicise a future event and send out invitations. To create an event, open the menu on the left-hand side of your Home page as discussed on page 126. Then, on iOS and Windows devices, select **Events** followed by **+Create**. On Android smartphones and tablets tap the icon shown on the right. Then select either **PRIVATE** or **PUBLIC** and fill in the details of the event such as title, location, date and time in the **Create Event** window, as shown below.

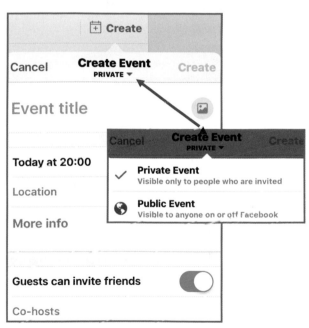

After tapping or clicking **Create** at the top right, the event appears full screen with options for you to **Edit** the details, **Invite** your friends or **Cancel** the event. After typing a few words to replace **Write something...**, select **Post** and the event will soon appear on your friends' News Feeds.

Pages for Businesses and Celebrities, etc.

You can set up a Facebook Page to promote a business, a cause, or a celebrity, for example. Open the menu on the left-hand side of the Home screen, as discussed on page 126. Select **Pages**, followed by **+Create** or **+Create Page**.

After selecting **Get Started** there are several stages to completing the Page including giving the Page a meaningful name and choosing a category from **Non–profit organisation**, **Local Business** or **Personal Blog**. You also have to enter your contact details and a link to your Website, if you have one. The Page can also include photos, videos, messages and a map showing your location, as well as several paragraphs of information about you.

Introducing Twitter

What is Twitter?

This chapter gives an overview of Twitter and what it's used for. Later chapters give more detailed instructions about setting up a Twitter account and how to use it.

Like Facebook, Twitter is a *social network*, allowing people to communicate worldwide over the Internet. Twitter is the second most popular social network behind Facebook and has millions of users, posting hundreds of millions of *Tweets* a day.

What is a Tweet?

A Tweet is a short text message, as shown below, which can be immediately viewed by an audience of thousands (or even millions of people if you're a celebrity or well-known person). Photos and other media can also be included.

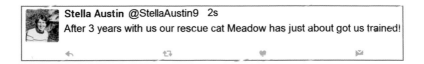

Stella Austin @StellaAustin9 2s
After 3 years with us our rescue cat Meadow has just about got us trained!

However, lots of ordinary people use Twitter to tell their friends and families what's happening in their lives. Many Web sites representing companies and organisations include a link to their Twitter pages where you can read their latest news. Celebrities and people with a lot of followers can use Twitter to get their message out to a wide audience. Twitter can also be used to host a debate or to gather support for a charitable cause.

Some of the essential features of Twitter are:

- Tweets, i.e. text messages of up to 140 characters.

- A Tweet can also include photos, videos, *stickers* (discussed in Chapter 12) and links to Web sites.

- Tweets are posted onto your own Home page and the Home page of *followers*.

- You can follow who you like and read their Tweets.

Tweets

The 140 Character Limit

Twitter is known for its 140 character limit on messages, similar to the 160 character limit on mobile phone text messages when Twitter was launched.

It was thought that by enforcing a limit of 140 characters, "Tweeters" would be more concise and organise their thoughts better — "brevity is the soul of wit". If you try to enter more than 140 characters, the message is truncated.

You don't have to use the full 140 characters. In the example of a Tweet below, **85** near the bottom right is the number of characters still available before the limit is reached. The spaces and the full stop in the Tweet all count as characters towards the 140 character limit.

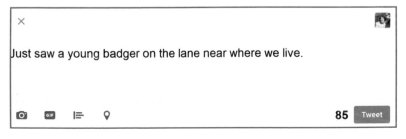

Relaxation of the 140 Character Limit

In 2016 Twitter relaxed the limit on the size of a Tweet by no longer counting photos, videos, GIFs and other people's quoted Tweets as part of the 140 characters. So you can use the full 140 characters for the text of a Tweet.

(GIF above is a file format for images and animations widely used on the World Wide Web).

Tweet Contents

The contents of a Tweet can be anything you like as long as it's not offensive, in which case the Tweet may be removed.

Posting a Tweet

When you post a Tweet it appears on your Home page and on the Home pages of all your followers.

Responding to a Tweet

A link at the bottom of a Tweet allows followers to post a reply. Friends and family who are currently online to Twitter, can, if they wish, post immediate replies. You can also *Retweet* or forward someone else's Tweet to the people following you.

Privacy

Normally when you post a Tweet, anyone can see it after searching for your name. The **Settings** feature in Twitter allows you to control who can see your Tweets. Opening the **Settings** menu and setting your Privacy on iOS, Android and Windows devices is discussed on page 153.

Followers

Twitter is based on the idea of *followers*. A follower is someone who is interested in reading someone else's Tweets. Although celebrities can have millions of followers, you could equally have a small group of friends or relatives following each other. The followers of important people or celebrities may simply want to read the Tweets out of interest, without expecting to take part in a two way conversation.

Twitter allows you to search for people by name or by their e-mail address and then start following them. Or you can invite friends to join Twitter via e-mail. Twitter also displays a list of celebrities you may wish to follow. You can choose who you want to follow, but you can't choose who follows you. You can *unfollow* someone you no longer wish to follow.

Direct Messages

Normally when you create a Tweet it's sent to all of the people who are following you. *Direct Messages*, however, are sent to a particular person or group of people who are following you, enabling you to have a private conversation. Unlike the 140 character limit on text messages a Direct Message can be up to 10,000 characters long and include a photo, as shown below.

A Zebra in Masai Mara

Twitter and Photos

A Tweet can include a link to a photo, as shown below. You can also insert videos and links to Web sites. As discussed later, photos and videos saved in your Gallery or Photos or Pictures folder on your device can be retrieved and inserted in a Tweet, as shown below.

Smartphones and tablets with built-in cameras can be used to take new photos and make videos to be included with a Tweet, as discussed later. Importing photos from external sources such as cameras, SD cards and flash drives is discussed in Chapter 13.

Stella Austin @StellaAustin9   15m

This jay came into our garden recently.

The Tweet appears as shown above on your Home page and on the Home pages of your followers.

Icons along the bottom of the Tweet, as shown above, allow you to **REPLY** to the Tweet, **RETWEET** it to someone else, **LIKE** the Tweet or post a *Direct Message* to start a private conversation with another person or group of people.

ofile Information

As discussed in more detail later, you can create a *Profile* for yourself or your business.

The Profile information appears in the lower half of the Twitter page as shown below.

Stella Austin
@StellaAustin9

Former R-R secretary and bank employee now mother, gardener, horse rider, cat lover and poultry keeper

♀ Sutton on the Hill

48 FOLLOWING   **212** FOLLOWERS

The Profile Photo

This is the small image above and can be up to 2MB.

The Header Photo

You can also include a Header photo of up to 5MB. This is the wide picture across the top of the screen shown above.

Biographical Information

Up to 160 characters of text are allowed, a location to say where you are and a link to a Web site.

Creating and editing your Profile is discussed in more detail in Chapter 11.

The Twitter Search Bar

You can look at all the Tweets on a particular subject by entering the keyword in the Twitter search bar across the top of the screen. Topical subjects such as **cycling**, for example, yield large numbers of the very latest Tweets.

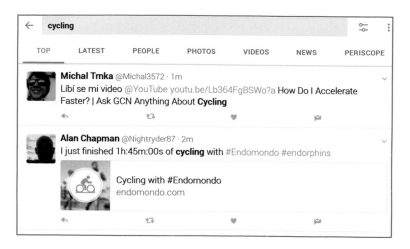

Hashtags

This is a hash symbol (#) you can place in front of an important keyword anywhere in a Tweet, as in the *#floods* example below. If readers of the message tap or click over the hashtag, lots of Tweets on the same subject are displayed. A hashtag must not include spaces or punctuation marks.

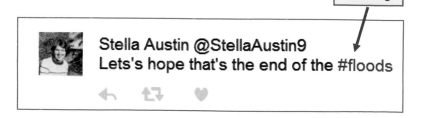

ome of the Main Features of Twitter

@

This is used to identify usernames in Twitter, e.g. **@johnbrown**. The username also acts as a link to the user's Profile.

Direct Message (DM)

DM is a private message between people who follow each other.

Follow

Tap or click the **FOLLOW** button next to someone's name to start receiving their Tweets on your Home page. You can follow anyone you choose and also **UNFOLLOW** them.

Hashtag

As discussed on the previous page, tapping or clicking the hashtag symbol displays all the other Tweets which contain the same hashtag anywhere within them.

Like

Tap the heart shaped icon at the bottom of a Tweet to show that you like a Tweet.

Mentions

When a **@username** appears anywhere in a Tweet, this is known as a *mention*. This allows you to see all the Tweets that include your **@username**.

Moments

Interesting current Tweets displayed by Twitter in categories such as news, sport, entertainment and fun. You can also create your own moments.

Notifications

This allows you to view all your recent mentions, follows, retweets and interactions.

Profile

This page displays your biographical information and photos as shown on page 134. It also shows the Tweets you've posted in your Profile Timeline.

Reply

A Tweet posted in response to a Tweet you've received. Tap the reply button on the Tweet. The reply starts off with **@username** of the person you're replying to.

Retweet

Forwarding to all of your followers a copy of a Tweet you've received from someone else.

RT

Used before a **@username** to give someone the credit when you forward a copy of a Tweet they've posted.

Timeline

The long list of Tweets on your Home page from the people you follow. The latest Tweets are at the top.

Trends

These are topics on Twitter which have been calculated by Twitter to be the most popular.

Tweet

A short message (140 characters or less) posted on the Internet to be viewed by your followers.

Key Points: Introducing Twitter

- Twitter is a social network based on *Tweets* or text messages of up to 140 characters.

- Tweets can also include photos, videos, GIFs and links to Web sites. Stored photos and videos can be inserted from your Gallery, Photos or Pictures folder.

- New photos and videos can be captured with the cameras built into smartphones and tablets.

- The Tweets you post appear on your Home page and on the Home pages of people who follow you.

- You can choose to follow anyone but you can't choose who follows you. You can set the *privacy* of your Tweets so they can only be seen by your followers.

- A *Direct Message* is posted to an individual person or group of people and allows you to have a *private conversation*.

- You can post a **REPLY** to a Tweet, **RETWEET** i.e. forward it to your followers or **LIKE** it, if appropriate.

- You can create a personal Profile with Header and Profile photos and 160 characters of biographical details about yourself.

- Tapping or clicking a hashtag such as *#climatechange* in a Tweet displays many other Tweets on a popular subject.

Getting Started With Twitter

Introduction

The procedure for getting up and running with Twitter is basically the same whatever type of device you are using — smartphone, tablet, laptop or desktop computer. The main steps common to all platforms are as follows:

- Sign up with your e-mail address and decide on and enter a Twitter username and password.
- Twitter will present a list of your e-mail contacts already on Twitter so you can select those you wish to follow.
- A list of your contacts who are not yet on Twitter is displayed and you can invite them to join.
- Twitter suggests a list of people you may wish to follow, including friends and also celebrities who are Tweeters.
- You can enter a personal Profile including a Profile photo and Header photo or image, if you wish.
- The Profile can be left blank during the set up process but may be completed and edited later.
- The Profile can also include a short description (up to 160 characters) of yourself or your company, etc.
- You can search for people and organisations on Twitter, look at their Profiles and decide if you want to follow them.

Installing the Twitter App

If necessary, you can download the Twitter app from the appropriate app store after tapping or clicking the icons shown below, in a similar way to downloading the Facebook app, as described in Chapter 2.

iOS

Android

Windows

Launching Twitter

Tap or click the Twitter app on the app screen or Home screen as shown below for Android and iOS (iPhone and iPad) devices.

iOS and Android

On Windows machines, open the Start menu tap or click the icon at the bottom left of the screen. Alternatively place a tile for Twitter on the Start screen, as discussed on page 19.

Windows

Signing Up

All you need to create your own Twitter account is a computer connected to the Internet and a genuine e-mail address. When you tap or click the Twitter icon on your apps screen shown on the previous page, the welcome page opens and you can either **Log in** to an existing Twitter account or **Sign up** to create a new one, as shown below.

Signing up involves entering your name and e-mail address and a mobile phone number. You are sent a verification code by text message to your mobile phone.

Your Twitter Username

After entering your full name, e-mail address and password, Twitter assigns a **Username** to you, based on your e-mail address. Your Twitter username always starts with **@**, as in **@timbrown**, for example. If the name has already been used, Twitter suggests other usernames based on your own name or adds the underscore character to your name as in **tim_brown**, for example. The username can only use upper and lower case letters, numbers and the underscore character. Spaces, punctuation marks, symbols and characters other than the underscore (_) cannot be used.

Following Your Contacts

Twitter suggests a list of people and organisations from your e-mail and phone contacts. Tap or click the icon as shown on the right and below to start following one of your contacts.

Contacts	
ALL CONTACTS	
B	
Babani Books	

Contacts	
ALL CONTACTS	
B	
Babani Books @BabaniBooks Publishing technical books since 1942. Low price paperbacks for all ages.	
L	
Liz Andrews @Flashholidays	
R	
Richard Gatenby @RichardGatenby	
S	
Stella Austin @StellaAustin9	

After you tap or click the icon on the right of a person or organisation, as shown above and on the right, the icon changes, as shown on the lower right, to show who you are following.

Following People With Similar Interests

You are asked to select your interests from a number of broad headings shown in the sample below.

Twitter then presents further sub-categories based on the choices you've made above. The subjects chosen here should help you to find interesting people to follow.

Sharing Your Location

You are then asked to agree to share
your location as shown on the right.
Twitter uses this to suggest accounts
for you to follow, some of which are
relevant to your home area, as shown below.

Popular near you

Paul Clement ✔
@PaulClement1972
Swansea City A.F.C Head Coach - Formerly FC Bayern
Munich, Derby County, Real Madrid CF, Paris Saint Germain,
Blackburn Rovers, Chelsea FC, Fulham FC.

Jeremy Clarkson ✔
@JeremyClarkson
I am a still small voice of calm and reason.

Derbyshire CC ✔
@Derbyshirecc
We're here to help you 8am to 8pm Monday to Friday and
9.30am to 4pm Saturdays

Searching for People to Follow

You can use the search bar in Twitter to look for
people or organisations to follow. On iOS (iPhone
and iPad) the search bar is displayed after tapping **Explore**
Explore at the bottom of the screen. To find
possible accounts to follow on a subject such as cycling,
for example, enter **cycling** or **#cycling** in the search bar.
(There should be no spaces or punctuation in the hashtag
#cycling.) The search produces a list of accounts of people
involved in cycling in various categories such as **People**,
shown on the next page.

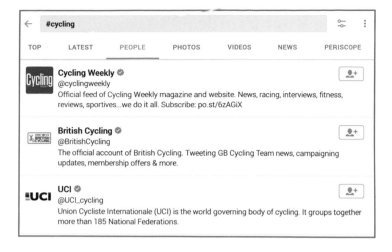

To find out more about a Twitter account, tap or click the name, such as **Cycling Weekly** shown above. This displays the Twitter Profile of the person or organisation. Then select **Follow** shown below to receive their Tweets on the stream of Tweets known as your Twitter Timeline.

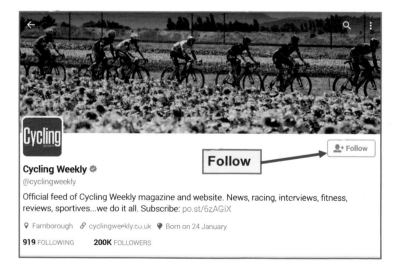

Creating Your Profile

During the sign up process you are given the chance to create your Profile. (If you prefer, you can leave it blank and edit your Profile at any time later, as discussed shortly).

You can select and upload a Profile photo from the Internal Storage of your smartphone, tablet, etc. This will help people recognise you if there are several others with the same name as you. If you don't include a Profile photo a blank, egg-shaped icon will appear against your name in Tweets as shown below.

Select **Not now** to postpone completing a stage of your Profile till later. You can also write a few words (up to 160 characters) about yourself before adding your birthday and *location*.

Viewing Your Profile

On Android devices select the small photo (or default icon) next to the word **Home** on your Home screen, as shown on the left below. Then select **Profile** from the pop-up menu.

On iOS (iPhone and iPad) devices tap the **Me** icon as shown the right. Your Profile is then displayed, showing any photos and biographical information you've already entered.

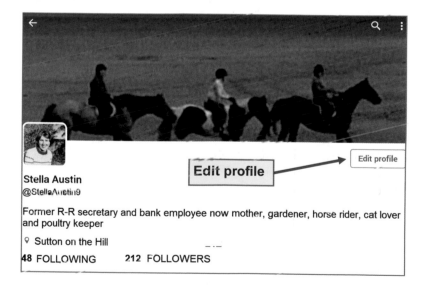

Editing your Profile is discussed on the next page.

Editing Your Profile

Select **Edit Profile** shown near the bottom of the previous page. This opens your Profile in editing mode as shown below. Now you can insert any photos or information omitted during the sign up process. Or you can change update or remove any existing information or photos.

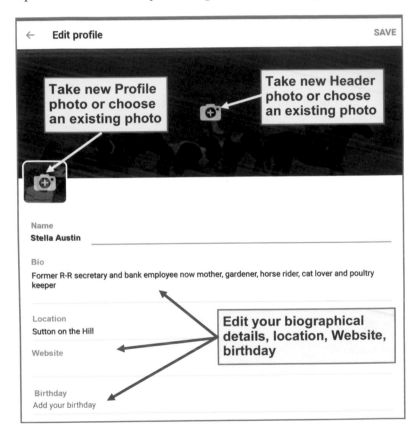

Finally select **SAVE** shown at the top-right above, to make the changes to your Profile permanent.

A Tour of Twitter

Although the screen layouts are slightly different, the basic functions and most of the icons are the same on Android, iPad and Windows tablets.

iOS (iPhone and iPad)

The Home page below shows your Timeline and all the recent Tweets you've sent and received from the people you're following. The main icons are along the bottom of the screen as shown below.

Android

The menu bar across the top of the Android Home screen, shown below, has several icons the same as the iOS version above. The slight differences are explained on the next page.

Windows

Microsoft Windows devices have broadly the same icons for accessing the main Twitter features, although on some versions they may appear vertically on the left-hand side of the screen, as shown below.

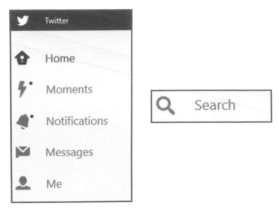

Functions of the Twitter Icons

Home

Displays your Home page or Timeline of all the Tweets you've sent or received from the people you are following.

Moments

This displays important events happening around the world, in categories such as **NEWS**, **SPORTS**, **ENTERTAINMENT** and **FUN**. This icon does not appear on iOS devices but users can create their own **Moments**.

Notifications

For example, informs you when new people are following you, when someone likes one of your Tweets or when one of your contacts joins Twitter.

Messages

These are the private **Direct Messages** (**DMs**) between two people who follow each other.

Me

Tap or click this icon to open your Profile and Timeline. On Android tap the miniature version of your Profile photo to open your Profile.

Tap to open profile

Home

New Tweet

Start a new Tweet. Replace **What's happening?** with your own text message of up to 140 characters.

Search

Presents the Twitter search bar allowing you to look for people or organisations to follow. Known as **Explore** on iOS. May also display a list of currently popular Tweets under **Trending now**.

Connect

Find people to follow on Twitter.

Signing Out of Twitter

To sign in with a different Twitter username and password, you first need to *sign out* as follows:

iOS (iPhone and iPad)

- Tap the **Me** icon at the bottom right of the screen, shown on the right.

- Tap the gear wheel icon as shown on the right. This appears on your Profile, under your Header photo.

- Select **Sign out** from the menu which appears.

Android

- From the top left of your Home screen, tap the miniature version of your Profile photo, shown on the right.

- From the menu which appears select **Settings**.

- From the **Settings** menu select **Sign out**.

Windows

- From your Home screen select **Me** to open your Profile.

- Select the people icon shown in the centre on the right, which appears below your Header photo in your Profile.

- Select **log out**` from the menu which appears.

Privacy

Twitter has a number of settings to protect the privacy and security of your Tweets.

iOS (iPhone and iPad)

- Open your Profile and select the gear wheel icon as described on page 152.

- Select **Settings** then **Privacy and safety**.

- Switch on the settings you require, such as **Protect my Tweets** and then select **Done**.

Android

- Select **Settings** as described on page 152.

- Select **Privacy and content** and switch on the privacy settings you require.

Windows

- Open your Profile, as described on page152, then select **Settings** as shown on the right.

- Then select **Security and privacy** followed by **Privacy and safety** and switch on the settings you require.

An extract from the iOS (iPhone and iPad) **Privacy and safety** settings menu is shown below.

.Key Points: Getting Started With Twitter

- Twitter apps are freely available from the app stores for all of the popular smartphones, tablets and PCs.

- You sign up with an *e-mail address*, *username* and *mobile phone number* (to receive a security code).

- Twitter usernames always start with the @sign and can only use upper and lower case letters, numbers and the underline character (_). Spaces and symbols are not allowed.

- You can enter your interests and biological information in your *Profile* during the sign up process or these can be left blank initially.

- Your Profile can be updated and edited at any time.

- Twitter uses your interests, Profile and *location* to suggest people for you to follow.

- Although the screen layouts may vary slightly, the main features and their icons are similar on all versions of Twitter – Android, iOS and Windows.

- The *search bar* can be used to find people to follow, perhaps after viewing their Profile. The use of the *hashtag* in a search finds all the Tweets and Tweeters on a popular topic you are interested in.

- Signing out of Twitter or deleting your Twitter account on a particular device does not remove the Twitter app or your Twitter username and password. You can sign in again whenever you want to.

Posting and Receiving Tweets

Introduction

When you first start using Twitter, you'll not have any followers and won't have posted any Tweets. Twitter will quickly suggest lots of people for you to follow, as discussed earlier. In fact you could use Twitter without any followers and without posting any Tweets. Simply use Twitter to follow celebrities, such as Jeremy Clarkson, with nearly seven million followers, as shown below.

However, if you want to post Tweets of your own, you need to get some followers – otherwise nobody will ever see your pearls of wisdom. You can use Twitter to have a dialogue with friends or family if you are all signed up to Twitter and following each other.

Finding People to Follow

If you want to follow a particular person or organisation, enter their name in the Twitter search bar, as discussed on page 144.

entering a name in the search bar, a long list of names
ople on Twitter with that name may appear. Obviously
rofile photo next to the name helps to identify the correct
erson or organisation as shown on page 142.

After selecting the person's name, their
Profile page appears, allowing you to tap
or click the **Follow** button, shown on the
right and below.

Then the **Follow** button shown above on
the Profile changes to **Following**, as
shown on the right. (Some systems just
display the ticked icon shown on the right).

Unfollowing

If you want to stop following someone, tap the **Following**
button on their Profile page and, if necessary, tap **Unfollow**
or **YES** from the menu which pops up on some systems.
Then the button on the Profile reverts to **Follow**, as shown
in the main screenshot above.

Posting a Tweet

Tap the New Tweet icon shown on the right, then start entering your text (up to 140 characters).

Text of your Tweet

@StellaAustin9 Riding Blade on the beach near Bamburgh Castle, Northumberland.

Stella Austin

Stickers

Edit photo

Camera

GIF

Question

Location

62 characters left out of 140 limit

62 | Tweet

Inserting Photos and Other Features

After entering the text of the message, you can enhance the Tweet in several ways using the four icons shown below. These are displayed at the bottom left of the New Tweet screen, shown on the previous page.

Photos and Videos

Tap or click the camera icon shown on the left above. This allows you to browse the Gallery, Camera Roll or Pictures folder on your device to select a photo or video to include in the Tweet, as shown on the previous page. The pencil **EDIT** icon on page 157 is used to crop the photo and experiment with different lighting and colour effects.

The two icons on the left below enable photos and videos to be taken with the cameras built into a smartphone or tablet and then included in a Tweet.

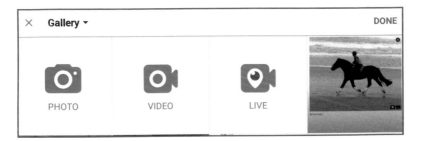

The **LIVE** icon shown above is used to broadcast a video *in real time*, i.e. as it happens, to all of your followers who are currently online.

GIFs

GIF is a file format used for graphical images and very short videos which keep repeating. Tapping or clicking the GIF button allows you to select from a large variety of GIFs and insert one to make the Tweet more interesting or amusing.

Questions

Selecting this icon allows you to ask questions of your followers. This could take the form of a question and answer session between people interested in a particular topic.

Location

The **Location** icon shown on the right and on page 157 displays a list of local businesses and places of interest, so you can tell your followers where you are. You can also add a precise map reference.

Stickers

The Sticker icon appears on a photo that you insert into a Tweet, as shown on the right and on page 157.

When you tap or click the Sticker icon, a large number of colourful images or *stickers* are displayed, as shown below.

Tap or click a sticker to insert it onto the photo, where it can be moved into its final position. In the example on the next page, the **LOL** sticker shown on the right has been added to the leaping cat photo. Finally tap or click **Save** at the top right.

Twitter has hundreds of stickers in different categories such as **Food & drink** and **Animals & nature**. Stickers are usually referred to as *emojis* and sometimes also as *emoticons*.

Emoji

An emoji is a small, colourful digital image, such as a smiley face, as shown on the previous page. It is intended to add amusement or emotion to a Tweet.

Emoticons

These were originally simple icons made from keyboard characters, used to express emotions.

:-)

Posting

When you've entered the text for a Tweet and inserted any extra photos, videos, stickers and GIFs, etc., tap or click the **Tweet** button shown on the right and on the bottom right of the screen shot on page 161.

Responding to a Tweet

The Tweet soon appears on your Home page and on your Profile/Timeline. The Tweet will also appear on the Home pages of all of your followers, as shown on the next page.

The follower can respond in various ways, such as:

- Post a *reply*.
- *Retweet* it to all of their followers.
- *Like* it for viewing later in their list of **Likes** and to tell the original Tweeter that they liked the Tweet.
- Send a ***Direct Message*** to their followers.
- Tap or click on a *hashtag* (e.g. *#climate*) within a Tweet to find other Tweets on the same topic.
- Tap or click on a link included with a Tweet to open a Web page.

When a follower receives a Tweet, it's displayed in their Home page as shown on the next page.

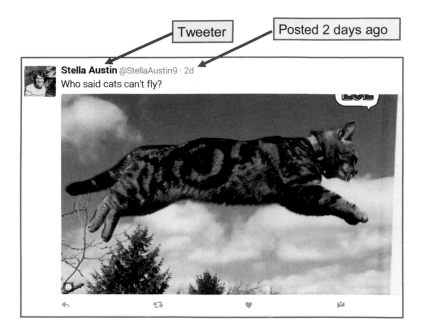

At the top of the tweet are the full name and username of the *Tweeter*, i.e. the person who posted the Tweet. Also shown is the time that has elapsed since the Tweet was posted, 2 days in this example. If followers are currently online, they can be reading your Tweets within seconds.

The follower's copy of the Tweet also includes a set of icons along the bottom, as shown in the main screenshot above and discussed on the next page.

The icons shown below appear on the follower's copy of a Tweet, as shown on the previous page.

The functions of the above icons are:

Reply to the person who posted the Tweet. The reply is also delivered to your followers and those of the originator.

Retweet, i.e. forward a Tweet you've received on to all of your followers.

Like a Tweet to tell the Tweeter you enjoyed reading it. Saves the Tweet in the **Likes** section of your Profile for viewing in the future.

Send a **Direct Message** to people on a list suggested by Twitter and perhaps start a discussion.

Replying to a Tweet

If you like a Tweet, you might wish to tap or click the heart -shaped icon shown above. The heart then turns red. The Tweet is then added to the list of **Likes** on your Profile/ Timeline. Tap or click the **Reply** icon shown above.

The originator's username appears on your screen next to a space ready for you to type your reply, as shown below.

> @StellaAustin9 That's pretty impressive Stella - what else can she do? Not a bad bit of photography either!
>
> 🗋 GIF   33 REPLY

After typing your reply, tap or click the **REPLY** button and the originator of the Tweet will quickly be able to view your reply on their Home page, as shown on the next page.

Receiving a Reply

The reply appears under the original Tweet, on the originator's Home page. A line on the left links the Profile photo of the original Tweeter and the Profile photo of the person replying.

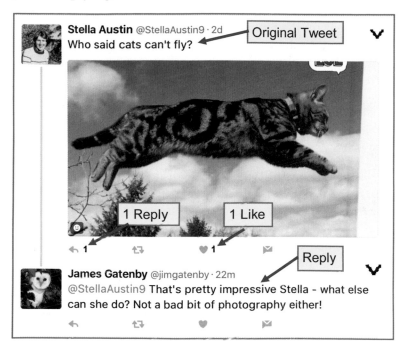

The original Tweet from Stella appears at the top, as shown above. The reply shown underneath includes the full name and username of the person replying, James in this example. This is automatically inserted by Twitter. The username of the original Tweeter, Stella, is also inserted automatically in blue preceding the reply, as shown below.

Retweeting

If you think a Tweet you receive will be of interest to your followers, tap or click the **Retweet** icon shown on the right. As shown on pages 163 and 164, this appears on the bottom of the Tweets from the people you are following. The retweeted Tweet will then appear on the Home page of all your followers.

The **Retweet** icon at the bottom of the Tweet displayed on the originator's page is highlighted and includes a **1** to indicate the Tweet has been retweeted, as shown below.

Using RT@username

Instead of using the **Retweet** button you can use the New Tweet window to forward a message to your followers. Type in **RT@username** to give credit to the original tweeter. Then copy the original message. You can modify the original Tweet and add text of your own, up to 140 characters for the whole Tweet.

Deleting Tweets

You can't delete Tweets that other people have posted. To delete one of your own Tweets, on Android and iOS devices, tap or click the arrowhead on the right of the Tweet shown on page 165. Then select **Delete Tweet**.

On Microsoft Windows, tap or click over a blank part of the Tweet and select the 3-dot menu button shown below. Then select **delete** from the menu.

Direct Messages

This is similar to a Tweet except that it's sent to selected individual users rather than to all of your followers. This allows you to start a *private conversation*.

- From the Home screen tap or click the **Messages** envelope icon shown on the right and on page 164.

- Select the New Direct Message icon at the top or bottom right of the screen as shown on the right (although the colours may be different).

- Select names from the suggested list or search for people or groups to receive the message.

- Select **Next** to start typing the message (up to 10,000 characters). You can also insert a photo, video, GIF or sticker as discussed from page 158 onwards.

- Finally tap or click the **SEND** button.

Shown below is a Direct Message including a photo sent to me from Stella. My Direct Message reply is shown in blue. At the bottom is a bar to start a new message, with icons to insert photos, videos, GIFs and stickers.

Key Points: Posting and Receiving Tweets

- A new Tweet can be up to 140 characters long and appears on your Timeline and Home page and on the Home page of anyone following you.

- The full name and the **@username** of the sender appear at the top of a Tweet. Tapping either name opens their **Profile**.

- A **Reply** icon appears on the Tweets you receive. Replies start off with the **@username** of the person posting the original Tweet.

- The **Retweet** button allows you to forward to your followers a tweet received from someone else.

- Alternatively enter **RT@username** of the original Tweeter and the text of their Tweet and any text of your own. This gives credit to the originator.

- A *hashtag* such as **#windfarms** in a Tweet makes it easy to find other Tweets on the same subject.

- A Tweet can include a photo, video and a *GIF* (a very short repeating video). Also a colourful *sticker* or *emoji*, plus a Web link and your location.

- A *Direct Message* is sent only to selected followers.

- The **Like** icon saves a copy of Tweet in your Profile and tells the originator that you liked their Tweet.

- You can't **Edit** your Tweets but you can **Delete** them from your Timeline and from your followers' Timelines.

13

Importing Photos and Videos

Introduction

Apps such as Facebook, Messenger and Twitter discussed earlier in this book allow you to insert photos and videos into the updates, tweets and messages that you post on the Internet. (The term photos will also include videos where used in the rest of this chapter).

Photos that you take using the built-in cameras on a smartphone or tablet are automatically saved on the Internal Storage of your device. This is usually referred to as the Camera Roll, Gallery or the Photos app. Facebook, Facebook Messenger and Twitter allow you to browse your Internal Storage to find and locate a photo, then insert it into an update, message or tweet.

However, you may have photos (and videos) that you wish to use with Facebook or Twitter, etc., that are currently saved on external media or devices. These external sources might include:

- Photos inside of a digital camera.

- Photos on SD cards and Micro SD cards removed from a digital camera.

- Photos stored on a USB flash drive or memory stick.

- Photos saved on a smartphone, tablet, laptop or desktop computer to be transferred to another device.

Connecting USB Devices

USB (Universal Serial Bus) ports are used to connect many external devices to smartphones, tablets and laptop and desktop computers. The *OTG cable* (On The Go), shown below has a *standard USB port* on one end and a *Micro USB connector*, on the other. The connector is inserted into the Micro USB charging port on a smartphone or tablet.

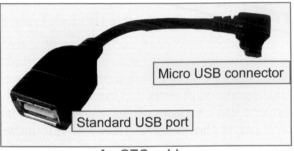

An OTG cable

The USB port on the OTG cable can be used to connect many external devices. These include *USB card readers*, into which you can insert the *SD cards* from digital cameras. Then the photos on the SD card can be transferred to a smartphone or tablet.

USB flash drives, also known as *memory sticks* and *dongles*, as shown below, may also be inserted in an OTG cable to transfer photos to your smartphone or tablet.

USB flash drive

USB ports are built in as standard to laptop and desk. computers and some larger tablets, so they don't need OT cables. So you can easily transfer photos from a computer directly to a USB flash drive. Then insert the flash drive into an OTG cable connected to your smartphone or tablet.

Similar OTG cables to that shown on page 170 for Android devices are also available for iOS (iPhone and iPad) devices and smaller Windows tablets and smartphones.

Importing Photos from a Digital Camera

Digital cameras are usually provided with a cable which has a USB connector or plug. This is normally used for charging the camera's battery. The cable can also be used for copying photos directly from the camera to a smartphone or tablet, without removing the SD card from the camera. Insert the OTG cable into the Micro USB charger port on the smartphone or tablet. Insert the USB connector on the camera cable into the USB port on the OTG cable. Then connect the other end of the charger cable to the camera. The smartphone or tablet detects the camera and you can then import the photos, as discussed shortly.

Digital Camera and USB Cable

Cards

The full size SD card shown below is the standard storage medium used in digital cameras.

Laptop and Desktop Computers

Modern laptop and desktop computers normally have a built-in *SD card slot* allowing you to import photos without the need for an OTG cable or card reader.

Android and Windows Smartphones and Tablets

The SD card can be removed from a digital camera and inserted into a USB SD card reader as shown below.

USB SD card reader

The card reader is connected to a smartphone or tablet using an OTG cable discussed on page 170. Then photos on the SD card can be imported and saved on the Internal Storage of a smartphone or tablet, as discussed shortly. The same USB SD card readers can be used on both Android and Windows devices. Larger Windows tablets and computers have the necessary built-in USB ports so an OTG cable is not needed.

iPhone and iPad

SD card readers are available for iOS (iPhone and iPad) devices, as shown below. These plug into the 8-pin Lightning port on iOS devices, or the 30-pin port on earlier devices, normally used for charging the battery

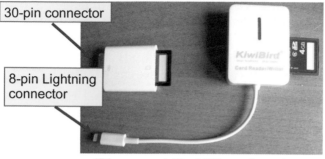

30-pin connector

8-pin Lightning connector

iPhone and iPad SD card readers

Micro SD Cards

Some tablets, such as the Samsung Galaxy range, have a built-in slot for a *Micro SD card*. An adapter the size of a standard SD card enables the Micro SD card to be used like a standard SD card in a digital camera. Then the Micro SD card, complete with new photos, can be removed from the adapter and inserted into the slot in the smartphone or tablet. The photo files can then be imported to the Internal Storage of the smartphone or tablet, where they will be available for use in apps such as Facebook and Twitter.

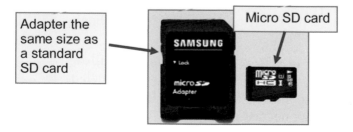

Adapter the same size as a standard SD card

Micro SD card

Transferring Photos

Android Smartphones and Tablets

Having connected an SD card or flash drive to the Android as discussed on the previous pages, the photos now need to be copied or transferred to the Internal Storage. Your Android may not have the necessary file manager app to import the files, but several apps are available for downloading free from the Play Store, discussed in Chapter 2. These include the USB Media Explorer, (previously known as the Nexus Media Importer), as shown below. This detects the photos and folders on the SD card or flash drive. Select **All Photos** to display the images as shown in the small extract below.

Tap to select the photos you wish to import or tap the 3-dot menu button shown on the right above and tap **Select All**. The **Copy** icon, shown on the right and above, saves the selected photos in **Photos** where they can be accessed by Facebook, Messenger and Twitter.

The **Share** icon shown on the right and above allows you to send copies of a photo to destinations such as Facebook, Messenger and Twitter, to be included in a new update, message or tweet.

iPhone and iPad

After you connect the card reader and SD card shown on page 173 to the iPhone or iPad, the **Import** icon pops up at the bottom of the screen, as shown on the right. Tap the **Import** icon and all the photos on the card are quickly displayed. Then tap to select the photos to be imported and tap **Import** or **Import All**. The photos are then copied to the iPhone or iPad, where they can be accessed by Facebook, Messenger and Twitter.

Microsoft Windows

As discussed earlier, flash drives can be connected to Windows devices either by using built in USB ports or on small smartphones and tablets, by an OTG cable. SD cards can be connected either by using a built-in card slot or by a USB card reader, if necessary via an OTG cable.

Windows tablets and smartphones, as well as laptop and desktop computers, use the *File Explorer* (formerly known as Windows Explorer) for managing files such as photos.

When you connect a camera, card reader or flash drive to a Windows tablet, the device is detected and appears with a name such as **Removable Disk (E:)** in the Windows File Explorer as shown at the top of the next page.

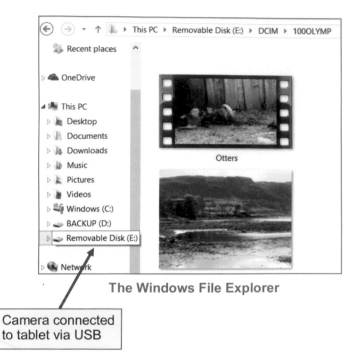

The Windows File Explorer

Camera connected
to tablet via USB

In the example above, a camera has been connected to a Windows device via a USB cable. As shown above in the File Explorer, the video and photo are in a folder called **100OLYMP**, within the **DCIM** folder on the camera's SD card. The camera has been automatically designated **Removable Disk (E:)**.

> ▸ **This PC** ▸ **Removable Disk (E:)**▸ **DCIM** ▸ **100OLYMP**

The File Explorer makes it easy to copy photos from the camera or flash drive or card reader to a folder on the Windows device (and vice versa). Simply drag and drop the photo over the new folder or use **Copy** and **Paste**. (Hold and release or right-click over a photo to display the menu).

Sharing Photos

Photos and videos stored on your device can be sent various destinations, such as Facebook, Messenger and Twitter. When you share a photo to an app such as Facebook, Messenger, Twitter or e-mail, the app opens, with the photo already included and a blank space ready to type a new update, message or tweet.

On Android and iPad, open the photo in the Photos app, then select the **Share** icon shown below. In Windows open the photo from the File Explorer to display the **Share** icon.

Android   **iOS(iPhone and iPad)**   **Windows**

Whichever system you're using, you are presented with a range of sharing destinations, including those shown below.

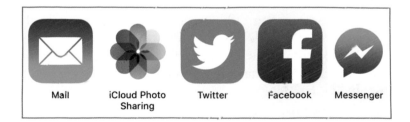

Mail   iCloud Photo Sharing   Twitter   Facebook   Messenger

Tap or click the required icon as shown above. The photo is displayed in the app such as Facebook, ready for you to type a message, replacing the words **Say something about this photo**. Finally tap or click **Post** to send the photo to your selected audience.

aging Photos Using a PC

ou have a laptop or Desktop PC, this can be used to anage the photos stored as files on a smartphone or tablet. his method uses the Windows File Explorer on the PC, which is powerful yet easy to use.

Using the battery charger cable supplied with a smartphone or tablet, connect the mobile device to a USB port on a PC. The mobile device appears in the File Explorer like an external device such as a flash drive, as shown below.

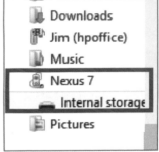

iOS(iPhone and iPad)   **Android (Nexus 7)**

The photos on the Internal Storage of a mobile device can be opened in the File Explorer on the PC, as shown below.

Right click over a photo to bring up the menu shown in the extract on the next page.

Edit	
Print	
Cut	
Copy	
Delete	

Apart from the option to **Delete** photos from a smartphone or tablet you can also use **Cut** and **Copy** on the PC to move or copy a photo, then **Paste** it into another folder. Alternatively use *drag and drop* to move or copy photos to a different location. These methods can be used to transfer photos between folders within the same device or between different devices such as PCs, tablets and smartphones.

Cloud Computing

This is another way to copy files such as photos between all your computers — smartphone, tablet, laptop or desktop. The Clouds, such as Dropbox, iCloud and OneDrive, etc., are actually Internet storage computers.

For example, to use Dropbox:

- Download the Dropbox app from **www.dropbox.com** to all your smartphones, tablets, laptops, etc.
- Create a Dropbox username and password.
- Save your latest photos and other files in the Dropbox folder on any one of your computers.
- Sign into Dropbox on any other computer. Your latest photos are automatically *synced* (copied) to all your computers. Photos can be copied from Dropbox to Facebook, Messenger and Twitter, for example.

y Points: Importing Photos and Videos

- Photos and videos taken using the built-in camera on a smartphone or tablet are automatically saved on the *Internal Storage* of the device .

- Apps like Facebook, Messenger and Twitter allow you to select photos from the Internal Storage and include them in an update, message or tweet.

- Photos and videos stored on external devices such as digital cameras, flash drives and SD cards can be transferred to smartphones, tablets or PC computers.

- Photos are transferred either by built-in USB ports on larger devices or by cables connected to the battery charging port on smartphones and small tablets.

- A file manager app such as the *USB File Explorer* is needed to import photos to Android devices. iOS devices have this capability built-in.

- The *Windows File Explorer* can be used to import photos on Windows smartphones, tablets and PCs.

- Android and iOS devices can be connected by cable to a PC computer for the management of their photos and the transfer of photos between different devices.

- Photos can be *synced*, i.e. copied automatically, between all your devices using a *cloud storage* system such as Dropbox, iCloud or OneDrive.

- The **Share** command can be used to send photos to Facebook, Messenger, Twitter, e-mail, etc. These apps are then opened ready to type a message.

- To share an old photographic print, take a photo with a smartphone or camera or scan it using an inkjet printer. Then upload it to Facebook or Twitter, etc.

Index